D1715713

The New York Times

LOOKING FORWARD

Clean Energy

THE ECONOMICS OF A GROWING MARKET

THE NEW YORK TIMES EDITORIAL STAFF

Published in 2019 by New York Times Educational Publishing
in association with The Rosen Publishing Group, Inc.
29 East 21st Street, New York, NY 10010

First Edition

The New York Times
Alex Ward: Editorial Director, Book Development
Brenda Hutchings: Senior Photo Editor/Art Buyer
Phyllis Collazo: Photo Rights/Permissions Editor
Heidi Giovine: Administrative Manager

Rosen Publishing
Greg Tucker: Creative Director
Brian Garvey: Art Director
Megan Kellerman: Managing Editor
Marcia Amidon Lusted: Editor

Cataloging-in-Publication Data
Names: New York Times Company.
Title: Clean energy: the economics of a growing market / edited
by the New York Times editorial staff.
Description: New York : The New York Times Educational Publish-
ing, 2019. | Series: Looking forward | Includes glossary and index.
Identifiers: ISBN 9781642820775 (pbk.) | ISBN 9781642820782
(library bound) | ISBN 9781642820799 (ebook)
Subjects: LCSH: Renewable energy sources—Juvenile literature.
| Clean energy industries—Juvenile literature.
Classification: LCC TJ808.2 C543 2019 | DDC 333.79'4—dc23

Manufactured in the United States of America

On the cover: Offshore wind farm turbines near Block Island, RI;
Chang W. Lee/The New York Times.

Contents

CHAPTER 2

Exploring the Options

CHAPTER 3

The Business of Clean Energy

CHAPTER 4

Clean Energy Controversies

Introduction

TODAY, the news is filled with dire warnings about climate change and its effects on our environment, as well as predictions of a future where we have run out of fossil fuels and don't have enough energy for the growing population of the world. But there is an area that also generates major news stories, even if they aren't typically front page headlines. Clean energy, meaning energy that comes from renewable resources such as wind, rain, sunlight, waves and geothermal heat, as well as bioenergy (including biomass and biofuels) and nuclear power, is a growing field. These sources of energy are potentially cleaner, healthier and better for the environment, and could possibly enable countries like the United States to be more energy secure because they will decrease reliance on foreign sources of energy such as oil.

The idea of clean, renewable energy is not only a reality, but is also becoming more mainstream. Thirty or so years ago, few Americans had solar panels on their homes to generate electricity. As of 2017, the U.S. was producing enough solar energy to power 10.1 million American homes. The cost of installing solar panels in individual homes has also decreased. As of 2017, wind power generated more energy — about 8 percent of the total U.S. power generating capacity — than any other renewable source. Windmills and wind farms, as well as solar arrays, are a common sight today. And scientists are continually finding new and innovative ways to generate energy. Even cars, which once relied solely on gasoline, are increasingly using electric batteries or hydrogen fuel cells instead of petroleum products.

As a business, clean energy is quickly becoming lucrative as renewable energy companies expand across the U.S. According to the

GEORGE ETHEREDGE FOR THE NEW YORK TIMES

Installing a solar panel on the roof of a house in Lewisburg, W.Va.

U.S. Department of Energy, the clean energy business sector generates hundreds of billions of dollars to the economy, and is expected to keep growing through the coming years. Jobs in the energy sector are growing, including jobs such as installing solar panels, constructing passive houses that use virtually no energy and designing systems for solar and wind power generation on a large scale.

However, clean energy has its downsides and its growing pains as well. Utilities are vying to develop these new technologies and generate revenue to replace what may be lost in traditional energy production from coal and natural gas. Some forms of renewable energy can have unanticipated environmental effects, such as large wind turbines being hazardous to birds. Nuclear power, which is often considered to be a clean source of energy, does generate radioactive waste that must be stored. And solar and wind power can only be completely effective if methods for storing the energy they generate can be improved so that there will still be power on days without sun or wind.

Clean energy, which is still developing, will have to address issues of supply and demand, the environment, human health and fluctuating markets. But in a world that is increasingly warming because of greenhouse gas emissions, and whose population is growing at a rate so rapid that its needs can't be met with traditional forms of energy, clean energy is no longer a case of wishful thinking. It is the future.

CHAPTER 1

Why Clean Energy?

There are many reasons to discover and develop cleaner sources of energy. The increasing population of the Earth means an increasing demand for energy. Many current energy sources are harmful to the environment as well as to human health. Climate change is linked to carbon emissions from fossil fuels, and these fuels themselves are a finite supply. Clean energy addresses these issues and is not only more sustainable in the long term for the planet, but often more cost effective as well.

Fuel Without the Fossil

BY MATTHEW L. WALD | NOV. 9, 2007

DENVER — Mitch Mandich proudly showed off his baby, a 150-foot contraption of tanks, valves, hoppers, augers and fans. It hissed. It gurgled. An incongruous smell wafted through the air, the scent of turpentine.

Mr. Mandich's machine devours pine chips from Georgia and turns them into an energy-rich gas, a step toward making liquid fuels. His company, Range Fuels, is near the front of the pack in a technology race that could have an impact on the way America powers its automotive fleet, and help ameliorate global warming.

"Somebody's going to hit a home run here," Mr. Mandich said. "We want to be first."

For years, scientists have known that the building blocks in plant matter — not just corn kernels, but also corn stalks, wood chips, straw and even some household garbage — constituted an immense potential resource that could, in theory, help fill the gasoline tanks of America's cars and trucks.

Mostly, they have focused on biology as a way to do it, tinkering with bacteria or fungi that could digest the plant material, known as biomass, and extract sugar that could be fermented into ethanol. But now, nipping at the heels of various companies using biological methods, is a new group of entrepreneurs, including Mr. Mandich, who favor chemistry.

They believe techniques borrowed from oil refining and other chemical industries will allow them to crack open big biological molecules, transforming them into ethanol or, even more interesting, into diesel and gasoline. Those latter fuels could be transported in existing pipelines and burned in existing engines without fuss. Advocates of the chemical methods say they may be flexible enough to go beyond traditional biomass, converting old tires or even human waste into clean transport fuel.

Mitch Mandich is among the entrepreneurs using chemical methods to try to make fuel from material like pine chips.

In Madison, Wis., a company called Virent Energy Systems is turning sugar into gasoline, diesel, kerosene and jet fuel, with the long-range plan of obtaining the sugars from biomass. In Ontario, Dynamotive Energy Systems is turning biomass into a form of oil, and in Chicago, a Honeywell subsidiary called UOP is doing something similar. In Irvine, Calif., BlueFire Ethanol is using acid to break down organic material for conversion to fuel.

Possibilities like these are coming to the fore at a time when rising oil prices have created an incentive to develop substitute fuels. Making them from biomass would be environmentally friendly in that, unlike standard gasoline or diesel, the fuels would not take long-stored carbon from underground and dump it into the air as carbon dioxide.

And unlike making ethanol from corn kernels, these techniques do not require significant amounts of natural gas or coal. Carbon dioxide, emitted in large volume when people burn fossil fuels, is the primary culprit in global warming.

Lately, these factors have resulted in a flood of investment capital into both biological and chemical techniques for using biomass. Experts consider both approaches promising, and they say it is too early to tell which will win.

"It's not obvious, and I don't think it will be obvious for a very long time," Andrew Karsner, the assistant secretary of energy for energy efficiency and renewable energy, said in Washington. His department is awarding grants to support both approaches.

Experts say it is possible that more than one type of plant will reach commercial success, with the ideal technique for a given locale depending on what material is available to convert to fuel.

Range Fuels favors pine chips and other waste from softwood logging operations, largely because there is so much of it. Logging in Georgia, for instance, leaves behind about a quarter of the tree. "Bark, needles, cones, we use all of it," said Mr. Mandich, chief executive of Range.

Range is a privately held company whose chief scientist, Bud Klepper, has been working on the two problems, creating gas from biomass

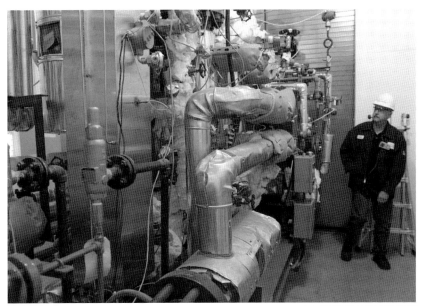

In Denver, Bud Klepper of Range Fuels is testing distillation equipment in the race for a viable alternative to fossil fuels.

and then converting it to liquid fuel, since the 1980s. The company is heavily backed by Vinod Khosla, a Silicon Valley venture capitalist who has turned his focus to energy investments.

Range broke ground this week on the first full-scale biomass-to-fuel plant in the United States, in Soperton, Ga. "Today marks the beginning of a new phase of our effort to make America more energy secure," the secretary of energy, Samuel Bodman, said at the event. The plant, its cost not publicly disclosed, is expected to produce 20 million gallons of ethanol a year, with more capacity to be added later.

In Georgia alone, enough waste wood is available to make two billion gallons of ethanol a year, Mr. Mandich said. If all that material could be captured and converted to fuel, it could replace about 1 percent of the nation's gasoline consumption.

Biomass of various types is abundant in every state, some of it gathered daily by garbage trucks. A study two years ago by the Oak

Ridge National Laboratory found that enough biomass is available in the United States to replace more than a third of the nation's gasoline consumption, assuming the economics can be made to work.

The Bush administration is counting on biofuels to help limit the growth of petroleum demand, and environmentalists routinely include such fuels in their forecasts as a way to reduce carbon dioxide emissions. But to date, no one has shown that fuels from biomass can be made profitably, even when competing with gasoline at $3 a gallon.

Daniel M. Kammen, director for the renewable and appropriate energy laboratory at the University of California, Berkeley, said, "I suspect we will have a trickle" of fuels from biomass in the next few years. But it will be only a trickle unless the government adopts quotas or offers additional support, he said.

Companies like Range that are trying to convert biomass by chemical methods follow one of two broad approaches. The first is to mix the material with steam to produce a gas known as synthesis gas, consisting of hydrogen and carbon monoxide. With additional processing, that gas can be converted to liquid fuels. The second technique does not break the material down as far, creating a product that resembles oil that can then be refined into liquid fuel.

Research papers and patents are flying these days as scientists struggle to improve these methods. As with oil refineries, the final stages typically produce a variety of chemicals, of varying value, and the trick is to maximize production of the desirable chemicals. "Everybody is dealing with a byproduct they don't want," said Arnold Klann, the chief executive of BlueFire.

Range Fuels is one of the companies that turn biomass into a gas before converting it to liquid fuel. The company wants to make ethanol, a form of alcohol, but its technique produces less valuable varieties of alcohol as well. Company scientists are tweaking their approach to maximize the ethanol yield.

The other day, laboratory technicians grabbed samples of a yellow liquid emerging from the machinery and swirled it like a suspect vintage of chenin blanc. An expensive chemical analyzer called a gas chromatography machine stood in the corner. By using it, engineers can calculate what changes in temperature, pressure and flow rates would work best to produce ethanol in a full-scale commercial venture.

Overseeing the operation, Mr. Mandich radiated confidence. "You can't have so many people at bat without hitting something," he said.

As the nation seeks to develop new types of fuel, Congress has leaned heavily toward ethanol made from corn kernels, and it is the only alternative fuel available today in large volume. Ethanol benefits from a tax break and a mandate that a significant amount of it be blended into gasoline.

Turning biomass into gasoline would be simpler, requiring no changes in the nation's cars or pipelines, but federal policy is tilting many research programs toward ethanol.

Range, for instance, could make any of several types of fuel from its pine chips. Asked whether the company chose ethanol for the 51-cent-a-gallon tax break, Mr. Klepper declared: "It's the American way."

Clean Power, Off the Grid

OPINION | BY DAVID J. HAYES | JULY 17, 2014

STANFORD, CALIF. — After years of hype, renewable energy has gone mainstream in much of the United States and, increasingly, around the world.

Enormous wind projects are moving ahead in oil- and gas-rich Wyoming, utility-scale solar projects are sprouting up in California and Nevada and tens of thousands of homeowners nationwide are installing affordable solar panels on their rooftops.

But many communities that need small-scale renewable energy remain out in the cold — literally and figuratively.

In Alaska, for instance, the vast majority of the more than 200 small, isolated communities populated primarily by native Alaskans rely on dirty, expensive diesel fuel to generate their electricity and heat. As in other remote communities throughout the world that have no grid to fall back on, diesel generators now provide the only reliable option for these desperately poor towns to meet their essential energy needs.

These villages buy and burn several hundred thousand gallons of diesel fuel per year in inefficient generators at costs that can approach $10 per gallon while spewing unhealthy fumes and soot. To ease their diesel dependence, some Alaskan villages have been able to secure financing to construct wind projects and small-scale, centralized electricity systems, known as micro grids. But the challenges of sizing and engineering these systems have slowed their development and installation. Even with generous support from the state and others, only about 25 of these systems have been installed over the past 20 years.

We can do better. In collaboration with government labs, the state of Alaska, private companies and investors, the United States is developing modular wind and solar energy systems that will work in isolated communities in Alaska, on island nations, in the African bush and elsewhere.

These systems are remarkably compact. Consider one that would provide enough renewable power for electricity, heating and cooling for a village of 100 to 200 people. It would include a refrigerator-size control center and a similarly sized container for storage batteries. The power would come either from one to five wind turbines, each about 100 feet tall with 20-foot-long blades, or from a solar panel array covering 700 square feet or more. Modern diesel generators would kick in when the wind wasn't blowing or the sun wasn't shining.

Bigger villages would simply scale up by adding on more modules. With standardized specifications, costs would drop as production ramped up and as the modular operations replaced the old headache-causing systems and their one-of-a-kind maintenance problems.

The Department of Energy's National Renewable Energy Laboratory has been working with the Department of the Interior and industry on the Remote Community Renewable Energy Partnership to make this happen. Drawing from the Department of Defense's successful deployment of small renewable energy- based systems to support forward-stationed troops, the lab is developing design specifications for a modular renewable energy system that aims to produce much cleaner energy, at half of today's costs. This would be accomplished by replacing 75 percent of diesel use for electricity and heat in the Arctic villages (relying primarily on wind power) and for electricity and cooling in the tropics (relying primarily on solar power).

On a parallel track, Energy Secretary Ernest J. Moniz recently announced a public-private collaboration called Beyond the Grid to leverage $1 billion in investments over five years to bring small-scale solutions to communities in sub-Saharan Africa. Both initiatives address the huge, debilitating energy deficit faced by millions around the world.

The potential payoff for cracking the code of providing smaller scale clean energy is huge. Diesel generators running around the clock in the tiny city of Wainwright, Alaska, and in many other similarly sized communities elsewhere in Alaska and in Africa and Asia, produce up to 22 pounds of carbon dioxide emissions for every gallon of diesel fuel consumed. In the Arctic, the climate impacts are magnified by added emissions of fine particulates known as "black carbon" — a powerful, short-lived warming agent that exacerbates the region's already-rapid temperature rises.

The economic and quality-of-life benefits that flow when cash-strapped communities have access to affordable and healthier clean energy are transformative. Just as the public-private partnership that developed and deployed cleaner-burning, efficient cook stoves has changed the lives of millions in Africa and Asia for the better, so also will these renewable energy systems.

Let's not leave these ideas on the drawing board. The United States will take its turn next April as the chair of the eight-nation Arctic Council, a forum of the nations that border the Arctic. In setting the council's agenda, the United States can make it a priority to bring practical and clean energy options to isolated northern communities.

Such an effort would put a humanitarian face on the country's commitment to address climate change. We would directly help our most energy-needy citizens, while opening up a new global market for American businesses and showing the world what innovative clean energy technology can do for the human condition, and our planet.

DAVID J. HAYES IS A VISITING LECTURER AT STANFORD LAW SCHOOL, AND WAS DEPUTY SECRETARY OF THE DEPARTMENT OF THE INTERIOR FROM 2009 TO 2013.

Paying in Pollution for Energy Hunger

BY KEITH BRADSHER | JAN. 9, 2007

BAHARBARI, INDIA — A toxic purple haze of diesel exhaust hangs over the rice and jute fields here in northeastern India, and bird songs are frequently drowned out by the chug-a-chug-a-chug of diesel generators.

Across the developing world, cheap diesel generators from China have become a favorite way to provide electricity. They power everything from irrigation pumps to television sets, allowing growing numbers of rural villages in many poor countries to grow more crops and connect to the wider world.

But as the demand increases for the electricity that makes those advances possible, it is often being met through the dirtiest, most inefficient means, creating pollution in many remote areas that used to have pristine air and negligible emissions of carbon dioxide and other global warming gases.

SCOTT EELLS FOR THE NEW YORK TIMES

A generator fueled in part by biomass in Baharbari, India.

"There has been a mushrooming of these decentralized diesel generators," said Ibrahim Rehman, a rural energy expert at the Energy and Resources Institute in New Delhi.

While many generators are purchased initially to power irrigation pumps, they have also opened up a huge new market for television sets, which in turn creates demand for even more diesel generators.

"You either want clean air or television" in many villages, said Nandita Mongia, the chief of the United Nations Development Program's regional energy program for Asia and the Pacific. In nearly all cases, television wins.

Rising prices for diesel fuel have improved the commercial potential of alternatives, but renewable energy sources have been in an often-losing race against smoke-spewing backyard diesel generators, and occasionally coal, to become the energy source of choice in outlying areas.

Renewable sources have made some inroads, including tiny hydroelectric dams for Himalayan streams, biomass generators for India

Ranvir Kumar Mandel, 22, built a bamboo hut in Baharbari to serve as a television repair shop. Before diesel generators, TV was not possible.

and Southeast Asia, solar-powered lanterns for India and Africa and rooftop water tanks in southern China.

But demand for electricity has been growing even more swiftly across the developing world, particularly in China and India.

When night falls here in Baharbari and countless stars blaze from an inky sky virtually uncontaminated by outdoor lighting, many of the thatch huts glow softly with the violet light of television screens, and occasionally a small bulb providing reading light for a child.

Three years ago, practically no one had a television set in this isolated community tucked between Nepal and Bangladesh. It is an area so remote and roadless that the only access is on foot or by bull-ock cart, after monsoon rains turn dirt paths into bogs that become impassable even for farm tractors.

Even so, half of the 1,000 households have TV, paying about 40 cents every few days to the owner of a diesel generator to recharge the batteries that power the sets. Ranvir Kumar Mandel, a slender 22-year-old, has built a bamboo hut here just to serve as a television repair shop.

"Before, there was no market," he said, sitting near a pile of mostly black-and-white sets to be fixed.

Lavish government subsidies for diesel, kerosene and other fossil fuels have held down prices in many developing countries and made it harder to introduce renewable energy technologies.

While entrepreneurs and organized crime syndicates frequently raise the subsidized price of kerosene and pocket the profits, it remains very cheap and is frequently mixed with diesel to reduce the cost of running generators. The mixture shortens the life of the generator, however, and can make pollution even worse.

Given the popularity of generators, perhaps the most promising alternative is a new type like the one at the edge of the village here that contributes much less to air pollution and global warming. It burns a common local weed instead of diesel, costs half as much to operate and emits less pollution.

The main material is dhaincha, a weed commonly grown in India to restore nitrogen to depleted soils. The dhaincha grows 10 feet tall in just four months, with a green stalk three inches thick. Wood from shrubs and trees is used when there is not enough dhaincha.

"Other villagers were surprised," said Ravindra Prasad Mandal, a village leader. "How was it possible that from dhaincha and wood, power was produced?"

For all its potential advantages, the toughest part of the project here has been to persuade change-resistant villagers to try it. Many projects fail in rural areas, development economists said, because governments or foreign aid organizations donate money or equipment without requiring any ongoing commitment. And they often threaten existing ways to obtain power, making it even harder to overcome resistance.

The biomass generator in Baharbari is owned by a collective of village residents, and has been supported by Hindus and Muslims alike. But local landlords, some with their own diesel generators that they rent out to charge batteries, have been wary.

Rice, jute and dhaincha fields in the village of Baharbari. Dhaincha, a weed that grows 10 feet tall in just four months, is a source of biomass.

The project has succeeded here partly because it has the active backing of one landlord family, the Sharans. Family members have gone on to successful business careers in big Indian cities and in Europe, and have dedicated themselves to helping their home village.

That makes it an unusual case, although the Sharans are trying to replicate it by setting up a school and training managers to establish similar cooperatives in nearby villages.

The biomass project has attracted interest and World Bank support because it appears to offer significantly cheaper electricity than diesel, at least at current prices. Another popular approach being tried in India and elsewhere — using solar energy to recharge lanterns by day — has run into difficulty even as diesel prices would seem to make it more competitive.

The problem is that prices for photovoltaic panels for solar energy have surged as governments in industrialized countries, especially Germany, have encouraged greater use of renewable energy, said Hemant Lamba, the coordinator of Aurore, a renewable energy service company in Auroville, India. "It's harder to do any solar energy projects in India," he said.

In mountainous countries like Nepal, development agencies have focused on designing very small, inexpensive hydroelectric systems to install in streams. But deforestation has denuded many hillsides in the Himalayas and elsewhere, causing rainfall to surge into streams much more quickly. A Japanese project in Bhutan was recently destroyed this way.

"The villagers shrugged and said, 'Nobody asked us, we knew every third year there would be a flood,'" Ms. Mongia, the United Nations energy expert, said.

Wind energy has found few applications in rural villages, because the turbines, even though far more capable than in the past, are still too expensive.

China has tried another approach: supplementing an expansion of electricity from coal-fired power plants with cheap rooftop solar water heaters that channel water through thin pipes crisscrossing a shiny surface.

Close to 5,000 small Chinese companies sell these simple water heaters, and together they have made China the world's largest market for solar water heaters, with 60 percent of the global market and more than 30 million households using the systems, said Eric Martinot, an expert on renewable energy at Tsinghua University in Beijing.

Wang Youyun, a 27-year-old lettuce farmer in Wangjiaying, a village of 3,000 people in southwestern China's Yunnan Province, bought one such hot water system a year ago for $360 and installed it on his family's roof next to a spot where ears of corn dry in the sunshine.

The village now has electricity, and some residents use it for water heaters, but Mr. Wang calculates that the solar system will pay for itself in two years. There is so much competition that even without government subsidies, the same size model now costs $330 and the price is still falling, he said.

The water heaters can be installed only on a sturdy, flat concrete roof, however, and not on the beautiful but fragile tile roofs that still adorn many of the houses in the village. The systems pose another drawback as well, Mr. Wang acknowledged: "If there is no sun for two or three days then there's no hot water."

Big conventional power plants, even those that burn coal, are often cleaner, safer and more efficient than crude household stoves and other small systems. So many economists say that the first step in developing countries should be the construction of power lines connecting as many villagers to national grids as possible.

Cooperation across national borders can help make this happen. Vietnam has made electricity available to 84 percent of its households, up from 50 percent in the early 1990s, partly by building a high-power line from China across Vietnam's impoverished northern highlands.

But power plants have actually closed in some of the poorest and most chaotic parts of the developing world, from Africa to dysfunctional states in India like Bihar, which includes Baharbari. Causes range from corruption to a failure of government-owned electricity boards to invest in maintenance and replacement parts.

Mohamad Aslam, 21, who sells time on a shared phone in Harwa, a village near Baharbari, said that he could remember lights shining outside homes when he was a boy, and when power from the national grid was still available. "It gradually decreased until it was gone: 10 to 12 hours a day, then five to six hours, then three to four hours and then there was no more," he said.

So for now, diesel generators remain the favorite choice of millions across the developing world — so much so that the International Energy Agency plans to assess the extent of their use as part of a detailed look next year at energy use in India and China.

Mohan Lal Yadav, the 55-year-old owner of a diesel station in Vehbra, a community of 4,000 people near Baharbari, calculates residents there have bought 100 diesel generators and 100 to 150 diesel-powered irrigation pumps in recent years. "It'll keep on increasing," he said.

Energy Idea for Mars Yields a Clue for Powering Data Centers

BY DIANE CARDWELL | NOV. 30, 2017

SUNNYVALE, CALIF. — As a scientist working for NASA in the 1990s, K. R. Sridhar developed a contraption that could use energy from the sun to transform the elements of the Martian atmosphere into breathable air or propulsion fuel.

It passed all its tests, but a planned mission to send it to Mars in 2001 was canceled and Dr. Sridhar moved on, looking to apply what he had learned to help stem climate change on earth instead.

"I came full circle — I was trying to make a really uninhabitable planet habitable," Dr. Sridhar, 56, said recently, holding a black-domed prototype of the shelved device at his Silicon Valley office.

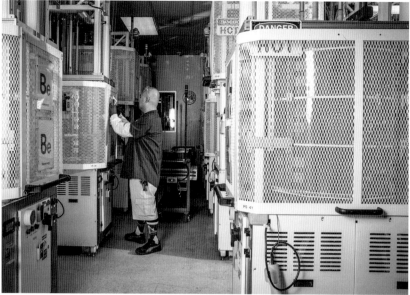

PETER PRATO FOR THE NEW YORK TIMES

Oliver Cruz, a technician, on the manufacturing floor at Bloom Energy, a producer of fuel cells in Sunnyvale, Calif.

"I was thinking, 'I can do something to make this planet a little more sustainable.' "

Almost two decades later, that thought has led to a fleet of fuel-cell generators that produce electricity through a chemical reaction. And with a recent deal for Dr. Sridhar's company, Bloom Energy, to install generators at a dozen data centers in California and New Jersey for Equinix, a leading operator, it is poised for a major expansion.

The aim of the deal, financed by a subsidiary of a deep-pocketed electric utility, Southern Company, is not only to create a reliable energy source for a power-thirsty industry, but also to help validate a technology that has struggled to gain mainstream acceptance.

What is striking is that the fuel cells are not running on hydrogen, like the ones long seen as a promising power source for cars. Instead, they use natural gas, which has become plentiful after a production boom over the last decade.

Even though they consume fossil fuels, the gas-powered cells have attracted the attention of some environment-minded policy-makers, investors and entrepreneurs because they release less of the heat-trapping gases like carbon dioxide than conventional plants. And they have been slowly finding fans among energy-conscious corporations — in Walmart stores, eBay data centers and Morgan Stanley's corporate headquarters.

Scott Samuelsen, director of the National Fuel Cell Research Center at the University of California, Irvine, said data centers could become an important market for fuel cells because the industry "appears to want to be more environmentally sensitive but more reliant on their own resources."

Part of the environmental appeal lies in their efficiency. Fuel cells are generally installed on site, so they do not need to burn extra fuel to compensate for energy lost over long transmission lines. In addition, they use less fuel per watt of power than conventional plants because they don't burn fuels to heat water or air to spin turbines.

That also makes them quiet, which has proved a surprising barrier to their acceptance among potential customers, Professor Samuelsen said. "It's hard for anyone to believe that they're making any power," he said. "It's not like a jet engine."

The innovations at Bloom stem from Dr. Sridhar's work on NASA's Mars exploration program when he was director of the Space Technologies Laboratory at the University of Arizona. Trained as a mechanical engineer in his native India, Dr. Sridhar arrived at the lab after getting a doctorate at the University of Illinois.

On the Mars project, he focused on using electricity to fuel chemical reactions among elements found on the Red Planet, even creating dirt capable of germinating a seed. Figuring that he should be able to reverse the process, he founded Bloom and worked on converting chemical energy to electricity using readily available fuels and conductors.

PETER PRATO FOR THE NEW YORK TIMES

K. R. Sridhar, the head of Bloom Energy, among its processing furnaces. After "trying to make a really uninhabitable planet habitable," said Dr. Sridhar, who once worked on a Mars project at NASA, "I was thinking, 'I can do something to make this planet a little more sustainable.'"

Eventually, he and his team hit upon a version of the current design of roughly 5-inch-square fuel cells fused together in stacks — each about the size of a half-loaf of bread and capable of powering an average home. The stacks are loaded into tubular metal casings before being enclosed in banks about the size of a refrigerator that can then be arrayed on the ground or a roof to run large facilities.

The equipment, produced at the company headquarters here with final assembly at a factory in Delaware, is simultaneously high- and low-tech. Each cell is made from a thin ceramic wafer that is mainly zirconia — a relative of the diamond substitute. In a process reminiscent of high school art class, the wafers are screen printed with chemical inks on each side in an automated sequence and then fired in kilns. They are sandwiched between metal plates, and the resulting structure is a solid oxide fuel cell that can operate at very high temperatures, about 800 degrees Celsius, or 1,472 degrees Fahrenheit.

At that temperature, when natural gas mixed with steam flows over one surface of the cell while oxygen flows over the other, a reaction results in the release of electricity, steam that is recycled through the process and carbon dioxide.

Equinix tested the Bloom cells at a data center in San Jose for 18 months before committing to the current arrangement, in which it will buy the energy under a 15-year power purchase agreement. The company, which runs more than 185 data centers on five continents, serves as a kind of cloud and network broker. It builds and operates facilities that provide space, power and cooling as well as work rooms, showers and a security system featuring a series of locked chambers like something out of "Get Smart." The client companies bring their own servers and other hardware to plug into more than 1,000 networks that connect them to customers and to each other.

The Southern Company, based in Atlanta, comes into the partnership because it has unregulated businesses that sell power nationwide. In this case, Southern buys the fuel-cell generators from Bloom and then, through a subsidiary called PowerSecure, sells the output to Equinix under a 15-year agreement.

The Bloom deal with Equinix and Southern is among the largest ever for a fuel-cell business, but Bloom faces competition from other providers, like Fuel Cell Energy, which is based in Danbury, Conn., and has a partnership with Exxon Mobil. It has won a number of recent contracts, which include installing and operating three fuel-cell projects for the Long Island Power Authority and one that will supply power for the Navy submarine base in Groton, Conn.

Indeed, the United States government has had a hand in the technology's development through grant programs at the Energy Department and a federal tax credit that expired at the end of last year.

The natural-gas fuel cells provide some environmental advantages over traditional power plants that run on fossil fuels: They use little water and release almost no harmful smog emissions. The Bloom cells can also run on biogas or hydrogen, which would make them even more environmentally friendly, given a steady supply of those fuels.

The usefulness of natural-gas fuel cells in reducing greenhouse gas emissions is a matter of some debate, however. Some environmentalists and public-utility officials say the fuel cells' emissions may be understated and question whether their carbon reductions are sufficient to warrant public subsidies.

Still, their emissions are well below the average for coal-fired plants. Bloom puts the emissions of its natural-gas cells in the range of 679 to 833 pounds of carbon dioxide per megawatt-hour, while coal plants released 2,252 pounds of carbon dioxide per megawatt-hour in the second quarter of this year, according to the Power Sector Carbon Index, an analysis published by the Scott Institute for Energy Innovation at Carnegie Mellon University. They are much closer to those of natural-gas plants, which, according to the index, averaged 938 pounds per megawatt-hour during the same period.

Though companies looking to power energy-hungry data centers have often sought out hydroelectric power, which does not depend

Randy Eoff, a manufacturing specialist, cleaning off the latest model at Bloom headquarters.

on fossil fuels and is generally inexpensive, fuel-cell technology is gaining traction, especially for customers who need an extremely steady power supply even during storms. For Tom Fanning, chief executive of Southern Company, the partnership with Bloom is part of a bid to take advantage of the technological advances that are upending the electric industry by allowing customers to make their own power, known as distributed generation.

"For 100 years, we have had a business model predicated on the notion of making, moving and selling electricity, essentially up to a meter," he said in a telephone interview. "We started seeing this make-move-and-sell model moving to the customer premises. And so we decided to become involved in this space."

The Connection Between Cleaner Air and Longer Lives

BY MICHAEL GREENSTONE | SEPT. 24, 2015

BACK IN 1970, Los Angeles was known as the smog capital of the world — a notorious example of industrialization largely unfettered by regard for health or the environment. Heavy pollution drove up respiratory and heart problems and shortened lives.

But 1970 was also the year the environmental movement held the first Earth Day and when, 45 years ago this month, Congress passed a powerful update of the Clean Air Act. (Soon after, it was signed by President Richard Nixon, and it was followed by the formation of the Environmental Protection Agency and passage of the Clean Water Act, making him one of the most important, though underappreciated, environmentalists in American history.)

NEAL BOENZI/THE NEW YORK TIMES

New York, 1966.

Since that time, the Clean Air Act has repeatedly been challenged as costly and unnecessary. As a fight brews over President Obama's new use of the law to address global warming, it's worth re-examining the vast difference the law has already made in the quality of the air we breathe, and in the length of our lives.

Numerous studies have found that the Clean Air Act has substantially improved air quality and averted tens of thousands of premature deaths from heart and respiratory disease. Here, I offer new estimates of the gains in life expectancy due to the improvement in air quality since 1970 — based on observations from the current "smog capital" of the world, China.

For several decades starting in the 1950s, China's government gave residents in the northern half of the country free coal for winter heating, effectively creating a natural experiment in the health impact of pollution. My colleagues and I recently compared pollution and mortality rates between the north and south of China and calculated the toll of airborne particulate matter, widely believed to be the most harmful form of air pollution, on life expectancy.

Applying that formula to E.P.A. particulate data from 1970 to 2012 yields striking results for American cities.

In Los Angeles, particulate pollution has declined by more than half since 1970. The average Angeleno lives about a year and eight months longer. Residents of New York and Chicago have gained about two years on average. With more than 42 million people currently living in these three metropolitan areas, the total gains in life expectancy add up quickly.

But some of the greatest improvements occurred in smaller towns and cities where heavy industries appeared to operate with few restrictions on pollution.

In 1970, the Weirton, W.Va.–Steubenville, Ohio, metropolitan area had particulate concentrations similar to current-day Beijing. A child born there today can expect to live about five years longer than one born in 1970.

More than 200 million people currently live in places monitored for particulates in 1970 and today. (The E.P.A. focuses on the most heavily populated or polluted areas of the country, which is why these calculations exclude approximately 115 million people.) On average, these people can expect to live an additional 1.6 years, for a total gain of more than 336 million.

Not all of these benefits came from Clean Air Act regulations. Other factors include local regulations and the shifting of relatively dirty industries abroad. But the Clean Air Act was a primary cause.

The history and impact of the Clean Air Act can serve as a valuable case study for countries that are struggling today with the extraordinary pollution that we once faced. In Northern China, where pollution is curtailing lives by an average of five years, the government has at last declared a "war on pollution." While enforcement is not perfect, the government has improved transparency and amended environmental protection laws to impose stricter punishments against polluters.

In India, pollution is abridging the average person's life by about three years. But the growing outrage has not yet coalesced into forceful action, although it's possible that pressure to take steps against climate change will also have an effect on improving air quality.

The hundreds of millions of life-years saved from improved air quality in our country didn't happen by accident or overnight. This happened because a collective voice for change brought about one of the most influential laws of the land.

As the United States and other nations continue to debate the costs of environmental regulation, they can do so with the knowledge that the benefits can be substantial. As proof, we need look no further than the five extra years residents of Weirton-Steubenville are living and the hundreds of millions of years gained by Americans throughout the nation.

Race Is On to Clean Up Hydraulic Fracturing

BY ERICA GIES | DEC. 4, 2012

PARIS — Hydraulic fracturing, or fracking, has raised fears around the world that the procedure needed to coax shale oil and gas out of tightly packed rock could cause pollution damaging to human health.

The process uses huge amounts of water, and environmentalists, landowners and others worry that drinking-water supplies could be contaminated.

"Our concern is with maintaining the quality of the water in our streams and preventing groundwater contamination," said George Jugovic Jr., president of Citizens for Pennsylvania's Future, an advocacy group.

But where environmentalists see risk, some entrepreneurs sense opportunity. With so much money at stake in this industry, businesses think that techniques that could ease concerns about water in fracking might prove valuable.

"Water is now emerging as a significant opportunity and risk for oil and gas companies," said Laura Shenkar, an expert on corporate water strategy and technologies and founder of the Artemis Project, a consulting firm based in San Francisco.

Fracking came into widespread use during the past decade after technological advances, particularly the ability to drill horizontally deep underground. To frack a well, millions of gallons of water, chemicals and tiny particles of sand, quartz or ceramics are pumped into buried shale rock formations.

The high-pressure liquids crack apart the rock, and the sand holds open the fractures. This allows trapped gas to flow into the well and up to the surface.

Gas companies add several chemicals to the fracking water, including biocides to kill bacteria from deep underground, scale inhibitors to reduce minerals that clog pipes and lubricants for the smooth operation of pumps and other machinery. Having these substances in the water creates pollution potential.

Some of the injected fluids flow back to the surface. Additional water that naturally occurs in deep rock also comes out with the gas. This water can create problems, too, because it contains a lot of salt and sometimes has radioactive elements.

Activists worry that the fracking process itself could contaminate groundwater. But evidence so far indicates that mismanagement of this wastewater is a greater threat.

Start-ups, venture capitalists and large companies, including Veolia and Siemens, see riches in water cleanup and are developing and testing various technologies. They are also working in other areas besides shale gas, including Canada's oil sands and the use of water to pressure oil out of wells.

One of these companies is Ecosphere Technologies of Stuart, Florida, which uses ozone as a disinfectant to clean water in a process called advanced oxidation. The treatment, which does not use chemicals, can both eliminate the chemicals typically used for bacteria control and scale inhibition during fracking and recycle 100 percent of the water, according to Charles Vinick, the company's chief executive.

Ecosphere says it has cleaned more than 2 billion gallons of water and eliminated the need for more than 1.7 million gallons of chemicals at approximately 600 oil and natural gas wells in U.S. shale fields since 2008.

It is now adapting its techniques to oil and natural gas liquids production, which are more profitable than shale gas at present. These operations also produce dirty water that needs to be cleaned and recycled, Mr. Vinick said.

Some companies have created "turnkey solutions" that allow gas companies to clean water on site and to validate the results by testing. The validation step makes it particularly attractive, Ms. Shenkar said.

One of the biggest players in this market is WaterTectonics of Everett, Washington. The company has a global licensing agreement with Halliburton, one of the largest oil services companies, for the frack water treatment market and other applications.

WaterTectonics uses electric current to bind together contaminant particles, allowing them to be filtered from the water. From 2009 to 2011, the company's staff and finances more than tripled, according to the company.

"Our system has been deployed on dozens of projects across the United States and most major shale plays," said TJ Mothersbaugh, WaterTectonics' business development manager. "There are also near-term plans to take it to offshore and other international applications."

While Mr. Mothersbaugh acknowledges that the recent drop in gas prices had affected his company of late, he remains a frack water bull. "The opportunity in frack water treatment is a very large market that is predicted to grow at an accelerated rate over the next 10 years," he said.

A few companies think that trying to reduce the enormous amounts of water used in fracking could be a moneymaker.

Daniel Choi, an analyst at Lux Research, a Boston-based a consulting firm that follows emerging technologies, estimates that by 2020, 260 billion gallons, or 984 billion liters, of water will be used to frack wells worldwide, a huge leap from the roughly 4.5 billion gallons this year.

Lack of water has already slowed shale gas drilling in drier states like Texas. During a summer drought in 2011, regulators suspended permits to withdraw water, limiting production in the Eagle Ford play, which is near San Antonio.

"The municipalities are starting to say that if we're having a drought and asking everyone to cut back, how can you possibly talk about using so much water?" Ms. Shenkar said.

But some companies are trying to prove this dire prediction wrong. GasFrac, based in Calgary, Alberta, is using a patented liquid petroleum gas gel instead of water as the primary fracking fluid.

After forcing the rock apart, the liquid fuel vaporizes and returns to the surface with the released natural gas. It can be recovered during natural gas treatment and sold as fuel or captured at the wellhead for reuse in fracking, said Nola Johnston, a sales and engineering assistant for GasFrac.

While technically a start-up, it's a monster baby. The company fracked 700 wells last year, mostly in Canada, in partnership with giant companies including Shell and Chevron. It's next big move will be into the United States, the company says.

How Grid Efficiency Went South

BY MATTHEW L. WALD | OCT. 7, 2014

ALMOST EVERY ROOFTOP solar panel in the United States faces south, the direction that will catch the maximum energy when the sun rises in the southeast and sets in the southwest.

This was probably a mistake.

The panels are pointed that way because under the rules that govern the electric grid, panel owners are paid by the amount of energy they make. But they are not making the most energy at the hours when it is most needed.

Solar panels thus illustrate how the rules add cost and reduce environmental effectiveness, critics say, because they are out of step with what the power grid actually needs from intermittent renewables like wind and sun, and from zero-carbon nuclear power.

THOR SWIFT FOR THE NEW YORK TIMES

Employees of SolarCity install photovoltaic panels on the roof of a house in San Leandro, Calif.

With the existing price structure, "we incentivize maximum power generation," said James Tong, the vice president for strategy and government affairs at Clean Power Finance, an investment firm. But in most parts of the country, there is plenty of electricity available from other sources in the morning and midday. Crunch time is late afternoon, when temperatures are higher and air-conditioners are working hard, and inefficient plants running on natural gas or even coal are cranked up to the maximum. That is obvious from the wholesale power market, where prices reach a peak in the late afternoon. But at that point, the declining sun is hitting the panels at an oblique angle, reducing power output.

"The needs of the grid may mean that they should be pointed west," more toward the setting sun, said Mr. Tong. That way, a bigger portion of their production would come at the hours when electricity was most needed. But their total production would be a bit lower, and that would hurt panel owners, at least under current rules.

The problem of solar panel orientation is simple compared with other emerging difficulties in the grid.

Some involve the difference between energy and power. The two terms are often used interchangeably, but they are distinct aspects of electricity. A quantity of energy is a bit like the number of gallons of gasoline in a fuel tank, and power is the horsepower of the engine. If four people want to drive from New York to Los Angeles with a load of luggage, 100 gallons might be enough energy for the journey. But if all they have is a motorcycle with a 500-cc engine, they lack the power to make the trip.

With the electric grid, the situation is similar. A small hydroelectric generator tapping a very large lake would produce a lot of energy, but its power is not enough to keep a lot of air-conditioners running. Likewise, solar and wind will produce a lot of energy, but the power they make often does not match the system's demand, so the contribution to its power needs may be much smaller.

The debate is over how to pay contributors to the grid so the system has an adequate amount of both energy and power. This is not a discussion likely to engage the ordinary consumer with a home electricity bill, but it is crucial to maintaining the stability of the system as the shift from fossil fuels proceeds to ones lighter on carbon.

Solar panels and especially wind turbines produce vast amounts of energy, but on their own schedule, when the sun is shining or the wind is blowing. The more conventional installations — coal, natural gas and especially nuclear plants — earn their keep by selling energy around the clock. Put enough wind and solar units on the grid during the hours when they are running and they flood the market and push down the hourly auction price of a megawatt-hour of energy.

Sometimes the price goes to zero. Oddly, it can go even lower. When demand is very low in the middle of the night and the wind is blowing hard, there may be too much electricity on the system and grid operators will charge generators that want to add more. Nuclear plants cannot quickly modulate their output so they are, in effect, fined for production. But wind farms still make money because they earn a tax credit for each kilowatt-hour they generate.

The problem is especially acute for nuclear reactors because their costs for fuel are roughly the same whether they are running or not. They are refueled on a fixed schedule, not when the uranium is used up. Their labor costs, mortgage costs and maintenance costs are roughly the same, too. But if the hourly price for energy is suppressed by wind and sun, suddenly the nuclear plants can't make enough money to keep running.

Thus some have already closed and more are threatened, even though carbon dioxide limits are unlikely to be met without them. Even relatively clean natural gas plants are hurt; they are generally on the margin, the first to shut when new solar comes on line.

The 40-year-old Robert E. Ginna Nuclear Power Plant on the shores of Lake Ontario in upstate New York is becoming an example of an emerging trend. Its income from selling energy is down because cheap natural gas and growing sources of renewable energy have depressed the market.

But the reactor provides a second service beyond energy: dispatch-able power, meaning the ability to support electric load on demand. And its owner, Exelon, argues that it is not paid enough for it.

"When we devote so many of our economic resources and our policies to the type of energy that produces power but not power on demand, we end up in a place where we start losing the megawatt we can control," said Joseph Dominguez, Exelon's senior vice president for governmental and regulatory affairs. "We've moved to a system focused on resources that provide energy when they want to."

Not everyone agrees. Most electricity markets have auctions not only for energy but also for capacity; utilities serving homes and businesses make what amounts to payments to assure that electricity will be available when needed.

"No planner, no regulator and no utility is going to leave them-selves capacity-short," said Ron Binz, an energy consultant, renewable energy advocate and former head of the Colorado Public Utilities Commission. What the renewables are really doing, he said, is "chang-ing the valuation of baseload plants," like nuclear and coal plants. A nuclear plant can barely change its output, and a coal plant can do so only within certain limits. A system that must compensate for rising and falling wind and solar generation makes the flexible plants, like those using natural gas, more valuable, he said.

And he and others noted the emergence of a substitute for generat-ing capacity: "Demand response" providers, which sign up customers willing — in exchange for a payment — to have their air-conditioners or industrial machines turned down or turned off by remote control at peak hours. These providers are paid by the companies that have to buy capacity.

Conventional generators, eager to maintain their revenue, per-suaded one big electricity market to limit the use of demand response.

The argument over how to value capacity and how to value energy has an echo in the debate over payments to the owners of solar panels at the retail level. In most states they get "net metering" — that is, if a utility charges them 15 cents a kilowatt-hour for energy, it pays them at the same rate when they produce. The payment relieves the panel owner of all the other costs of electricity — maintaining capacity for hours when the sun does not shine, and moving the electricity from the producer to the consumer, all wrapped into the retail rate that consumers traditionally paid, and that now the utility pays the panel owner.

The homeowner with panels on the roof may think he or she is disconnected from the system, when in fact the connection has become stronger, making the household a supplier as well as a consumer of energy, and a consumer of all the grid's other functions, like capacity, transmission and distribution.

All the various generators connected to the grid — now including rooftop solar, and "microgrid" owners who generate on their own but use the grid for backup — are going to have to share some of the costs, predicted Martin

E. Shalhoub, manager of business development for ABB's Power Consulting business. But with utilities trying to maintain profitability, and green advocates trying to encourage solar and other distributed generation, the argument will be complicated.

"Not everybody is going to be happy," he said.

Cleaner China Coal May
Still Feed Global Warming

BY KEITH BRADSHER | JUNE 17, 2011

LIANYUNGANG, CHINA — The six massive silos standing beside this industrial port in northeastern China hold seemingly contradictory promises: They could help improve the quality of China's polluted air, but they might also contribute to faster global warming.

The silos, which are scheduled to start operation in July, are designed to blend cleaner-burning imported coal with China's own high-polluting domestic coal, which is contaminated with sulfur and dust.

Coal blending will produce a mixture that will help electric utilities meet China's steadily tightening environmental regulations. It will also increase the efficiency of coal-fired plants by slightly reducing the quantity of coal needed. Burning less coal means less greenhouse gases emitted.

But critics argue there is a darker side to cleaner coal.

"Anything that makes coal more cost effective, like blending, which is only enabling China to burn more coal, is bad news for the global struggle against carbon emissions," said Orville Schell, the Arthur Ross director of the Center on U.S.-China Relations at the Asia Society in New York.

The Chinese government's decision this month to import more coal in order to lessen power outages — and control rising coal prices — ensures that blending will increase rapidly.

Industry executives are quick to tout the practice's environmental benefits. Blending "is a sound solution to reducing greenhouse gas and pollutants emissions from coal-fired power plants," said Howard Au, the director and chairman of Petrocom Energy Ltd., which owns the blending facility here.

But environmentalists worry that by reducing the amount of sulfur and dust emitted from burning coal, blending makes coal more acceptable in the short-term and stalls the conversion to cleaner or renewable fuels. They say coal blending strengthens the case for companies — and countries — that want to continue to rely on coal for decades.

"Does it help with acid rain? Yes," said Allen Hershkowitz, a specialist in Appalachian coal fields at the Natural Resources Defense Council, an environmental group based in New York. "It hurts us when it comes to global warming."

Coal remains a particularly dirty form of electricity generation when it comes to producing climate-changing gases.

The global warming calculus for coal blending is less clear. Blending makes it easier to feed a power plant with exactly the right coal mixture at which its boilers work most efficiently. This means the plant can burn less coal and emit less greenhouse gas. How much less — and how does that improvement compare with switching to other fuels — varies a lot depending on the power plant and the coal it burns without blending. Better operating efficiency at the power plant helps offset the cost of blending, which can add up to 4 percent to the price tag of the coal.

China does not just have an ancient civilization, it also has a lot of very old coal. Much of it has been tightly compressed over millions of years. That has pluses and minuses.

Chinese coal releases a lot of heat when burned and has very little moisture left, two very desirable features, according to coal traders. But Chinese coal deposits also contain a lot of sulfur as well as so-called fly ash — dust that is not combustible and contributes to particulate air pollution.

China also has some deposits of young coal which has fairly low heat content and requires blending before it can be burned.

China has the third-largest coal reserves, after the United States and Russia, and consumes more coal than any other country. It accounted for nearly half the 7.3 billion metric tons burned around the world last year.

Four-fifths of China's reserves, however, do not comply with the country's standards for industrial use, according to the government-run China Coal Research Institute. Complicating matters, the China's environmental regulators have signaled plans to reduce further the allowable levels of sulfur.

China led the world last year in clean energy investments, with $54.4 billion, according to a study by the Pew Charitable Trusts. But coal is still China's dominant energy source, accounting for 73 percent of electricity capacity.

Because coal-fired plants run day and night — while alternatives like wind turbines and hydroelectric dams only run when enough wind or water is available — coal accounted for 83 percent of electricity generation last year.

China has led the world in recent years in the construction of high-efficiency coal-fired power plants. These plants heat water to higher temperatures and pressures than earlier designs, so that less coal is burned to produce the same kilowatt-hours of electricity. But the newer power plants need coal of a precise makeup, making it even harder for China to rely exclusively on domestic coal fields.

To meet the needs of the new plants, China has gone on a twin binge of importing coal and buying coal mines abroad. Wood Mackenzie, the global energy consulting company, predicts that Indonesia will be the world's fastest-growing exporter of coal in the next five years because of Chinese demand.

While coal blending facilities may provide a short-term environmental benefit, they also make it possible for countries like China to plan on consuming a lot more coal for decades into the future.

People have been blending coal for more than a century, often in surprisingly simple ways. Richard Elman, the chairman of the Noble Group, one of the world's largest commodity companies, is skeptical of newer blending technologies. He says bulldozers have been roughly mixing different grades of coal at power plants and mines for years.

A single coal mine may have different qualities of coal in different seams, and will often stir them together with bulldozers before shipment so as to provide a mixture that better meets the customer's specifications, he said.

In the United States, big engineering companies like Bechtel and the Roberts & Schaefer subsidiary of KBR have been designing elaborate systems of conveyer belts that take coal arriving by rail and barge and distribute it to various stockpiles, blending it along the way.

The most elaborate approach, developed in Europe and put into effect here, is to build a series of silos, each containing a different grade of coal. A large conveyor belt and scales are mounted underneath the silos. Coal from each silo is sprinkled onto the conveyor belt, then the mixture is dropped into rail cars, ships or a storage yard.

"It's not easy for this new technology to be accepted, so I'm using my network because I believe this would be good for the country," said Li Anqing, the retired top administrator of Lianyungang's big coal port, who is now the general manager of the operation here.

Bob Williams Jr., the vice president for sales and marketing at Roberts & Schaefer, said that using specially built silos for blending coal is an unusually expensive approach, and would barely be considered except at large coal ports. But Mr. Au said that the blending cost per ton using silos, about $5, had not changed for the last several years.

By contrast, coal prices have doubled in the past five years, to $130 a ton in China for coal with high heat content. So blending costs have halved as a percentage of the overall cost of coal. That reduction in relative costs, combined with tighter regulations in China aimed at reducing acid rain, have increased its attractiveness.

"Blending didn't make sense prior to 2003 as prices of coal were low," Mr. Au said. But now, Petrocom is making plans for dozens of coal-blending facilities in China, to accommodate a flood of imports that could last for decades.

Public Lives; A Windmill Builder, Tilting at the Old Ways

BY COREY KILGANNON | JAN. 30, 2003

ROMPING GIDDILY in the snow at the windmill farm he built here in central New York, Bill Moore bears little resemblance to the Yale-educated consultant he once was, working in Manhattan on the financing of nuclear power plants and other utilities.

After Mr. Moore, 46, quit Wall Street several years ago to develop wind farms, his old finance colleagues chuckled at him and his tree-hugging obsession.

Mr. Moore's company, Atlantic Renewable Energy, has developed five of the seven commercial wind farms operating in the Eastern United States, but they have had problems finding buyers in the energy market. He has spent the last three years trying to build the biggest windmill farm in the East, which has yet to break ground or attract investors. His former colleagues wondered if he was building windmills or just tilting at them.

Then, this month, Gov. George E. Pataki issued a directive that a quarter of the state's electricity supply should come from so-called green sources, like wind or solar or hydroelectric power, within the next decade. This would require suppliers to buy a percentage of "clean energy" at a slightly higher price than conventionally produced energy.

Now it seems as if Mr. Moore might have the last laugh.

"No one knows we're up here doing this," he said. "It's like we're in a vacuum sometimes. And that's fine. We have a good head start."

On a quiet, snowy hilltop in Madison, a town 40 miles southeast of Syracuse with about 2,800 residents, Mr. Moore walked among seven huge windmills and beamed like a happy father.

"You can actually feel it sucking the energy out of the wind," he said.

Each 1.5-megawatt induction generator weighs 65 tons. Each has a three-blade rotor on a hollow cylinder. The sleek white windmills over-head, about 330 feet tall, emit a gentle, whooshing noise. These are made in Denmark and cost $1.8 million each to buy and install.

The windmills have an other-worldly look, like something out of a science fiction movie.

"They have an elemental quality," Mr. Moore said, staring up at a windmill as the wind spun its blades against the blue-gray sky. "When the light hits it right, the white blades against the blue sky, the setting sun, it can take your breath away."

Maybe, but certainly not now. Mr. Moore has a calm, quiet speaking style, but when it comes to talking windmills he seems powered by the endless energy of the wind.

The governor's order could bring investors and push power companies to buy the electricity, which costs a bit more than electricity produced by gas, oil, coal or nuclear power. "It could really jump-start this whole industry," he said.

He spoke while steering his Land Rover through Madison, a Mozart clarinet quintet on the radio. He braked for some snowmobilers.

Madison County is a region dense with trailer parks and pickup trucks and backyard smokehouses stuffed with deer meat. In much of this region, industry has left and dairy farmers have come upon hard times. But the region still has its elevated plateaus and strong lake winds and a big demand for power.

Mr. Moore grew up in Greenwich, Conn. As an undergraduate at Yale, he wrote his senior paper on wind and solar energy. He also got a master's in economics from Yale, specializing in financing environmental energy plants.

On most weekends he flies back home to Maryland, to the old farmhouse he is renovating. Most of his weekdays are spent on the road, which has kept him a bachelor, he said. A couple years ago, his girlfriend gave up on him. He took 27 trips to Costa Rica in a year; she took her dogs and moved to Colorado. He has put 135,000 miles on his Land Rover in the last two years.

Mr. Moore's romance with windmills began with an epiphany in 1997.

"I was in Denmark and I walked up to a megawatt-scale generator and I knew I had to start building these."

He spends much of his time trying to get his largest project, called Tug Hill, in Lewis County, east of Lake Ontario, off the ground. The farm would have 160 windmills stretching across 10 miles. The challenge, he said, is winning the trust of local landowners, to lease space for the farms.

"When I first started visiting farmers, we'd sit down and I'd start scribbling notes in my book," he recalled. "I soon realized that you don't walk into a farmer's kitchen and start talking business. They want to talk for an hour, just for the conversation."

As for the aesthetic debate, Mr. Moore said, "It's really in the eye of the beholder."

"There is certainly a visual impact," he said. "But when you look at the side effects of producing power, the aesthetic issue is pretty far down the list."

The complaints come from the weekenders, who want quaintness, antiques and scenery.

"It's my Starbucks rule," he said. "If there's a coffee chain in town, you know those are the people who will be complaining."

Sun Is Part of the Plan for Greener Hempstead

BY MATT MABE | APRIL 6, 2008

THE TOWN OF HEMPSTEAD deploys park officials in a fleet of electric cars to patrol its beaches and parks. A windmill atop a landfill-turned-recreation area circulates water in a nearby pond. The town is even testing hybrid garbage trucks to reduce their exhaust.

"We want to go entirely green here," said Kate Murray, the town supervisor.

But the most ambitious of Ms. Murray's environmental plans sits right above her head: 256 shiny blue panels on the town hall's roof. They make up a 40-kilowatt photovoltaic — solar energy — system to power her office and a conference room next door.

In January 2006, the town began using solar systems to deliver electricity to some of its buildings, using state subsidies to cover most of the equipment and installation costs. But while town government views itself as a leader in reducing pollution, some experts say solar technology is still largely inefficient and not worth the cost to taxpayers.

A recent audit by the state comptroller's office commended Hempstead for putting the system in place. It said the town should save $419,000 in energy costs over the estimated 50-year life of the panels. Hempstead paid a quarter of the $336,000 price tag, with the New York State Energy Research and Development Authority covering the difference.

But Howard C. Hayden, a retired physics professor at the University of Connecticut who has specialized in alternative energy methods, is skeptical about the broader use of solar energy because he says its cost inefficiency does not justify the use of taxpayer dollars to pay for it. "It's a scam," said Dr. Hayden, the author of "The Solar Fraud: Why Solar Energy Won't Run the World," "and the public will be victimized financially and intellectually."

It will take more than 40 years to pay for the equipment and its installation, the audit report notes. And Hempstead will have to raise its own money to wire further government buildings.

Town officials said, however, that while protecting taxpayers' pocketbooks is important, they did not undertake the project for cost savings alone. "Our first and foremost goal is to reduce our carbon footprint and keep our planet clean," said Michael Deery, a town spokesman.

The audit says the system at town hall will reduce carbon dioxide emissions by 1,250 tons over a half-century — the equivalent of what 220 cars would produce over the same period.

Ms. Murray, who said her commitment to the environment is her highest priority, is buoyed by the audit's findings. The town has held several seminars on solar energy to explain to residents how it can benefit their homes and businesses and how rebates can help defray the costs.

Peter Ray, 64, who lives in Levittown, attended one of the seminars and was persuaded to buy the technology for his home. He said he installed a $54,000 system, 60 percent of which the Long Island Power Authority and the state subsidized. "I would recommend it to anybody," said Mr. Ray, who said he expected a return on the investment from saved energy costs in three and a half years.

According to the United States Department of Energy, renewable sources — like water, wind and sun — accounted for only 7 percent of total national energy consumption in 2006. The reason is the cost of making the technology efficient, Dr. Hayden said. (The national average retail price of electricity is about 10.5 cents a kilowatt-hour, while energy from solar cells costs 18 to 40 cents a kilowatt-hour.) "They are trying to be leaders," he said of Hempstead officials, "but they are going to lead us down a very expensive path."

Nevertheless, William Reynolds, a spokesman for the state comptroller's office, said, "We cannot downgrade the importance of being able to reduce emissions produced by burning fossil fuels."

Whether private citizens choose to switch to solar or not, Ms. Murray is determined for her government to set an example.

"As focused as we have been on efforts to go green, we have been just as aggressive in pursuing the grants to pay for them," she said. "We're pretty successful in everything we ask for."

CHAPTER 2

Exploring the Options

There are many types of cleaner energy, from solar and wind power to more exotic ideas such as algae, sugar and even power generated from deep space. As concerns about fossil fuels and nuclear energy increase, scientists are searching for even more ways to generate energy without damaging the environment or creating health hazards. The methods discussed in this chapter are only the beginning, as new energy sources are being experimented with every day.

Kelp Farms and Mammoth Windmills Are Just Two of the Government's Long-Shot Energy Bets

BY BRAD PLUMER | MARCH 16, 2018

OFF THE COAST of California, the idea is that someday tiny robot submarines will drag kelp deep into the ocean at night, to soak up nutrients, then bring the plants back to the surface during the day, to bask in the sunlight.

The goal of this offbeat project? To see if it's possible to farm vast quantities of seaweed in the open ocean for a new type of carbon-neutral biofuel that might one day power trucks and airplanes. Unlike the corn- and soy-based biofuels used today, kelp-based fuels would not require valuable cropland.

Of course, there are still some kinks to work out. "We first need to show that the kelp doesn't die when we take it up and down," said Cindy Wilcox, a co-founder of Marine BioEnergy Inc., which is doing early testing this summer.

Ms. Wilcox's venture is one of hundreds of long shots being funded by the federal government's Advanced Research Projects Agency-Energy. Created a decade ago, ARPA-E now spends $300 million a year nurturing untested technologies that have the potential — however remote — of solving some of the world's biggest energy problems, including climate change.

This week at a convention center near Washington, thousands of inventors and entrepreneurs gathered at the annual ARPA-E conference to discuss the obstacles to a cleaner energy future. Researchers funded by the agency also showed off their ideas, which ranged from the merely creative (a system to recycle waste heat in Navy ships) to the utterly wild (concepts for small fusion reactors).

Consider, for instance, wind power. In recent years, private companies have been aiming to build ever-larger turbines offshore to try to catch the steadier winds that blow higher in the atmosphere and produce electricity at lower cost. One challenge is to design blades as long as football fields that will not buckle under the strain.

At the conference, one team funded by ARPA-E showed off a new design for a blade, inspired by the leaves of palm trees, that can sway with the wind to minimize stress. The group will test a prototype this summer at the Department of Energy's wind-testing center in Colorado, and ARPA-E has connected the team with private companies such as Siemens and the turbine manufacturer Vestas that can critique their work.

While there are no guarantees, the researchers aim to design a 50-megawatt turbine taller than the Eiffel Tower with 650-foot blades, which would be twice as large as the most monstrous turbines today. Such technology, they claim, could reduce the cost of offshore wind power by 50 percent.

Or take energy storage — which could enable greater use of wind and solar power. As renewable energy becomes more widespread, utilities will have to grapple with the fact that their energy production can fluctuate significantly on a daily or even monthly basis. In theory, batteries or other energy storage techniques could allow grid operators to soak up excess wind energy during breezy periods for use during calmer spells. But the current generation of lithium-ion batteries may prove too expensive for large-scale seasonal storage.

It's still not clear what set of technologies could help crack this storage problem. But the agency is placing bets on everything from novel battery chemistries to catalysts that could convert excess wind energy into ammonia, which could then be used in fertilizer or be used as a fuel source itself.

At the summit, Michael Campos, an ARPA-E fellow, also discussed the possibility of using millions of old oil and gas wells around the Midwest for energy storage. One idea would use surplus electricity to pump pressurized air into the wells. Later, when extra power was needed, the compressed gas could drive turbines, generating electricity. A few facilities like this already exist, though they typically rely on salt caverns. Using already-drilled wells could conceivably reduce costs further.

"This is a very early stage idea," Dr. Campos told the audience. "I'd love to hear from you if you have ideas for making this work — or even if you think it won't work."

Other projects focused on less-heralded problems. A company called Achates Power showed off a prototype of a pickup truck with a variation on the internal combustion engine that it hoped could help heavy-duty trucks get up to 37 miles to the gallon — no small thing in a world in which S.U.V. sales are booming. Several other ventures were tinkering with lasers and drones to detect methane leaks from natural gas pipelines more quickly. Methane is a far more potent greenhouse gas than carbon dioxide.

Looming over the conference, however, was the murky future of the agency itself. The Trump administration, which favors more traditional sources of energy such as coal, has proposed eliminating the agency's budget altogether, arguing that "the private sector is better positioned to advance disruptive energy research."

So far, Congress has rejected these budget cuts and continues to fund the agency. But the uncertainty echoed throughout the conference, even as Rick Perry, the energy secretary, sent along an upbeat video message lauding the agency's work — a message seemingly at odds with the White House's budget.

"We are at a crossroads," Chris Fall, the agency's principal deputy director, told the attendees. "But until we're told to do something different, we need to keep thinking about the future."

When Congress first authorized ARPA-E in 2007, the idea was that private firms often lack the patience to invest in risky energy technologies that may take years to pay off. Many solar firms, for instance, are more focused on installing today's silicon photovoltaic panels than on looking for novel materials that might improve the efficiency of solar cells a decade from now.

Because energy technologies can take years to reach fruition, the agency does not yet have any wild success stories to brag about. By contrast, a similar program at the Pentagon created in the 1950s, the Defense Advanced Research Projects Agency, or DARPA, can fairly claim to have laid the groundwork for the internet.

Instead, ARPA-E's defenders have to cite drier metrics, like the fact that 13 percent of projects have resulted in patents, or that its awardees have received $2.6 billion in subsequent private funding.

In a review last year, the National Academies of Sciences, Engineering and Medicine concluded that "ARPA-E has made significant contributions to energy R&D that likely would not take place absent the agency's activities." The report added, "It is often impossible to gauge what will prove to be transformational."

BRAD PLUMER IS A REPORTER COVERING CLIMATE CHANGE, ENERGY POLICY AND OTHER ENVIRONMENTAL ISSUES FOR THE TIMES'S CLIMATE TEAM.

Gleaning Clues on Sunny Days From the Clouds

BY DAVID FERRIS | OCT. 23, 2012

CARLOS F. COIMBRA knew from the outset that he would have to crack the code of clouds. As an engineering professor new to the University of California's campus in Merced, he led a successful drive to get 15 percent of the school's power from an array of solar panels.

But clouds, wandering and capricious, had foiled his efforts on two occasions by casting sudden shadows, forcing the school to rely on conventional power instead. To neutralize the clouds, he would have to track them.

So Professor Coimbra, a Brazilian-born expert in fluid mechanics with a flair for computer modeling, tried a new kind of forecast. The campus would make better use of sun power if he could figure out exactly when a puffy drifter would arrive overhead. He wrote a

Carlos F. Coimbra with equipment used to track cloud cover, on a rooftop at the University of California, San Diego.

computer algorithm to project how clouds move and change shape as they move across the sky — one of the most complex and chaotic phenomena on earth, influenced by an endless set of variables.

Now, six years later, Professor Coimbra, 44, and his collaborator, Jan P. Kleissl, 37, have created a forecasting engine that they say is 20 to 40 percent more accurate than the model in common use. Weather, energy and power grid experts said that the innovation could accelerate the adoption of renewable energy, save billions of dollars in energy costs and help turn cloud-watching from an idle pastime into a vital and profitable part of the weather forecast.

"I can't tell you what's going to happen at 4:23 p.m. on a Sunday," said Professor Coimbra, whose forecasts extend to seven days but with decreasing accuracy. "But I can tell you what will happen between noon and 6 today."

Potential cost savings are drawing the interest of companies that build and operate solar-power plants, as well as utilities and grid operators. Each bets a bottom dollar on when the sun will come out tomorrow. A fine-tuned forecast makes it easier for utilities and grid operators to use the sporadic power of sun and wind when they are available, giving renewable energy a reliability close to that of a fossil-fuel or nuclear power plant.

Furthermore, it could help utilities predict exactly when homeowners will turn on their air-conditioners in the summer, which could reduce the power grid's need for backup power plants.

As it saves money in energy markets, the technology could also shake up the world of weather forecasting by providing greater resolution. Such data could give airports a firmer window of when storms will arrive and leave, resulting in fewer flight delays.

It could tell farmers when to expect the first frost, or when a rainstorm will hit, reducing the need to pump water for irrigation. A precise prediction could guide the maneuvers of forest firefighters, project the path of bioterror attack or pinpoint the path of a tornado.

Melinda C. Marquis, the renewable energy project manager at the government's Earth System Research Laboratory in Boulder, Colo., speculated that this technology, born to serve renewable energy, might end up changing our relationship with weather. "Any improvement that we make here for renewable energy will be very, very important, in some cases more important, for other sectors of the economy," she said.

But the forecasts are likely to find their first application at solar and wind farms. Currently, the caprice of weather makes electricity more expensive for producers and consumers of utility-scale renewable power. Traditional weather forecasts aren't accurate enough to predict when the sun will poke through the clouds on a partly overcast day and make mistakes in estimating the length and strength of high winds.

To compensate, some solar and wind farms maintain large, expensive banks of backup batteries to store surplus energy and release it when needed. Grid operators scramble to buy power on the spot market when weather-related energy sources fall short, buying power for 10 to 100 times more than they would if they bought a day ahead, according to Manajit Sengupta, a scientist who leads solar-forecasting efforts at the National Renewable Energy Laboratory. A perfect forecast for wind, if it represented 20 percent of the power supply, would save $1.6 billion to $4.1 billion a year, according to several studies.

The spikes and troughs of wind and sun, known in the power industry as "ramp events," cast another shadow for plant operators. Abrupt changes can damage equipment and cause backup batteries to fill or drain too quickly, shortening their life spans, and, with them, the useful life of the plant.

The test sites that Professor Coimbra and Professor Kleissl use are small affairs, made up of a few small, spindly weather instruments that reside on rooftops and alongside solar arrays at facilities in Washington State and throughout California, from Davis down to San Diego.

The most important instrument is a fisheye camera that points at the sky, taking photos of five square miles every 30 seconds. This device, engineered by Professor Kleissl, tracks cloud speed and creates a forecast for the next three to 20 minutes.

For longer time frames, Professor Coimbra's number crunching takes over. A self-learning computer algorithm, it digests dozens of measurements — solar irradiance, wind speed, satellite images, soil moisture — and sorts out which are relevant and which are noise. Such modeling has been used to predict the behavior of other complicated systems, like the interaction of molecules or the swings of the stock market, but it has never been used to create hyperlocal forecasts.

In the two years since Professor Coimbra moved to University of California, San Diego and started a partnership with Professor Kleissl, their team of graduate and postdoctoral students has grown from seven to 25 as research money comes in.

The California Public Utilities Commission issued a $1.5 million grant to improve forecasts of San Diego's ever-changing coastal fog, and the California Energy Commission gave $1 million to help Professor Coimbra develop an accurate model of the thick, ground-clinging fog of the Central Valley.

The two researchers are awaiting approval of projects to model the weather above the military's large solar installations in and near the Mojave Desert, where the North American monsoon can create violent summertime storms.

So far, however, the only commercial application is at a 22-acre field of kiawe trees in Hawaii, at the site of a proposed five-megawatt power plant in Kalaeloa, Oahu. The builder, Scatec Solar North America, hopes that an accurate profile of the "solar resource" will compensate for the island's vulnerabilities: bright sun, sudden squalls and a small, outdated power grid that cannot handle large spikes in the power supply. An accurate forecast would eliminate the cost of backup batteries and make it easier to find investors, the chief executive, Luigi Resta, said.

Back in California, the California Independent System Operator, which manages the state power grid, is about to compare the forecasts of the University of California, San Diego, against its own, a model based on temperature, time of day and historical records of energy use that has not been tweaked in decades. If the San Diego model is more accurate — say, correctly guessing that a region uses 900 megawatts of electricity on a hot summer day instead of 1,000 — "then that's some money" that will be saved by ratepayers, said Jim Blatchford, the smart grid solutions manager.

Professor Coimbra's prognostications could even give racecar drivers the inside track. A private company, Forecast Energy, has hired him to create a model that could, for example, inform a driver's team during inclement weather exactly how wet the track will be for the next 10 laps — data that could determine the crucial decision to use slower, safer wet-track tires or faster, dry-track tires to win the race.

How solar forecasting will be used as it matures is anyone's guess, but it could be handy for anyone who needs a more exacting snapshot of the weather — like Professor Coimbra himself, who keeps a careful eye on distant thunderheads as he rides his motorcycle along Interstate 15. As he does so, he ponders the sort of question that perplexes farmers, pilots, backyard grillers, and anyone else whose fortunes depend on the whimsical schedule of clouds.

"Is the rain going to get there before I get to Point B?" he asked. "Or can I go 50 miles more?"

A Storage Solution Is in the Air

BY ERICA GIES | OCT. 1, 2012

PARIS — Renewable energy sources like wind and solar have a problem: When the wind stops or it is night, they stop generating power. That drawback has focused minds on the question of how to store electricity generated by intermittent sources.

The global market for energy storage services could be worth as much as $31.5 billion in 2017, according to Brian Warshay, an analyst at Lux Research, a consulting firm based in Boston.

The ultimate goal of grid operators is to match the power they deliver to the needs of their customers. Utilities have traditionally increased production from gas-fired power plants when needed to smooth supply and demand, but energy storage systems could, in theory, do the job more quickly and cleanly. Depending on where the storage is situated, it could also reduce the need for new transmission lines.

With increased interest has come investment: Venture capitalists and governments are funding research into batteries, pumped hydro-electricity, flywheels and compressed air.

Battery technologies have received much of this attention, but compressed air is also moving forward.

In an ideal storage system, all the energy put in can be extracted later. When air is compressed, however, the work that goes into compression produces heat as a side effect. In early compression storage systems — technically known as diabatic — this heat has been lost into their surroundings, making them less efficient.

Current experimental systems aim to be more efficient by retaining or recovering the heat. Some, known as isothermal, use a coolant to absorb it, keeping the air at a near constant temperature. The coolant, stored separately, is tapped later to give back the energy through a heat exchange system. Others, known as adiabatic, allow the temperature of the compressed air to rise and fall, using the air, when hot, to warm heat storage units that retain energy within the system.

SustainX, based in Seabrook, New Hampshire, is set to build a pilot isothermal plant capable of storing and releasing up to two megawatts of power, making it the largest demonstration of the technology to date. At the same time, a German consortium is planning a truly grid-scale project — initially up 90 megawatts — based on the adiabatic approach.

Isothermal and adiabatic are terms from thermodynamics that promise perfect efficiency, with no energy loss. In practice, each system must make compromises that lower the efficiency rate to 50 to 70 percent.

SustainX's facility, a follow-up to a 40-kilowatt demonstration plant, is funded partly by a $5.4 million U.S. government grant under the 2009 American Recovery and Reinvestment Act and partly by venture capital. Richard Brody, the company's vice president of business development, said it could start test operations by next June, though it would have only an hour or two of storage capacity and would not initially be intended to supply power to the grid. "Its goal will be to validate and demonstrate the technology to our engineering team and to customers," he said.

Both SustainX and the German consortium are seeking to improve on the diabatic technology used in existing utility-scale facilities in Huntorf, Germany, and McIntosh, Alabama. In these systems, the operators use surplus power from the grid when demand is low to pump air at high pressure into underground salt caverns, expelling the byproduct heat into the atmosphere. When energy is needed on the grid, the air is released and reheated by burning gas before being sent through turbines to generate electricity.

In the SustainX isothermal process, a fine mist of water is used as the coolant. When grid power is needed, the compressed air is passed back through the heated water to recover the stored energy before being fed to the turbines.

A venture capital-funded start-up, LightSail Energy in Berkeley, California, has built two prototypes using similar technology — both LightSail and SustainX use specially built containers rather than underground caverns to store compressed air.

Meanwhile, General Compression in Newton, Massachusetts, is working on a near-isothermal system using salt cavern storage, like the early diabatic systems. General Compression and its partner ConocoPhillips are developing a project in western Texas.

Mr. Warshay, who has written a review of SustainX, said he expected that the project would provide valuable data. "Because it's D.O.E.-funded, they will have to publish their performance data, which will help the industry as a whole understand the technology's capabilities," he said, referring to the U.S. Department of Energy. And because the technology is built with off-the-shelf components, the market will be able to estimate its cost, he added.

The German consortium, meanwhile, is seeking to develop a related adiabatic technology in which the temperature of the compressed air would be allowed to vary within a range of 600 degrees Celsius to 40 degrees Celsius, or 1,112 degrees Fahrenheit to 104 degrees Fahrenheit. Heat generated by the compression process would be stored in large, ceramic- filled concrete pressure vessels. A first planned prototype plant would have a capacity of up to 90 megawatts.

The consortium, called Adele — the German acronym for adiabatic compressed air energy storage — includes the power utility RWE, the construction and engineering contractor Züblin, the German Aerospace Center and the U.S. conglomerate General Electric. It is currently negotiating for German government funding and hopes to have the demonstration plant operational by 2019.

Like the older diabatic plants, Adele would use salt cavern compressed air storage — its planners are focusing on a suitable site near Stassfurt, a city in the state of Sachsen-Anhalt — but the consortium says the addition of the ceramic-concrete heat storage units should raise the efficiency of the whole system to above 60 percent.

An advantage that SustainX and LightSail have over Adele is that their technologies are not site-specific. They can be placed wherever they are needed: next to a wind farm, for example, or a factory that generates its own power.

But they are also more costly: Roland Marquardt, research and development manager for RWE Power on the Adele project, said pressurized air storage cannot be done more cheaply than by using Adele's large-scale process.

The growing percentage of renewable generation in the electricity system, particularly in Germany, requires thinking big, he said. "Three-digit- megawatt scale is what we are looking for to have significant impact," Mr. Marquardt said.

Still, he added, the future will likely offer different roles for different technologies.

Mr. Brody of SustainX warned that given the low price of natural gas in the United States currently and policy frameworks that are not creating strong incentives, "it will be very difficult for any storage technology to compete in conventional applications."

SustainX is therefore eyeing other markets, where fossil fuel prices and policy incentives are more conducive to economic success. The company also plans to target more creative applications.

"We see substantial value, both in the United States and in other markets, where grids are facing constraints that cannot be addressed through traditional generation or T and D assets," he said, referring to costly investments in transmission and distribution lines.

Electrical Charge Helps Sun Shine on Solar Panels

BY HILLARY BRENHOUSE | OCT. 12, 2010

MONTREAL — At first glance, the most logical place to establish a large-scale solar-power installation is in the desert, where the blistering sun is not impeded by cloud cover and much of the land is not fit for cultivation. But these dry, inhospitable stretches of sand, with their frequent dust-filled blasts of wind, pose a big problem for photovoltaic panels, which are significantly less effective when covered with dirt.

Even a thin layer of grit — four grams per square meter, or one-seventh of an ounce for almost 11 square feet — can decrease a panel's solar power output 40 percent or more. Dust in the Negev, for example, accumulates an average 0.4 grams per square meter per day; 10 days of uninterrupted buildup would reach that level. And dust levels are even higher in other popular solar sites across the Middle East, Australia and India.

Fortunately, a team of U.S. research scientists has found a potential solution, based on technology developed with NASA for missions to Mars and presented in late August at the 240th National Meeting of the American Chemical Society in Boston.

The solution may be a self-cleaning coating for photovoltaic panels that repels dust with the help of electrical charges. It is the only technology for automatic dust removal "that doesn't require water or mechanical movement," said Malay Mazumder of the Department of Electrical and Computer Engineering at Boston University, who directed the research.

Washing down large-scale installations is often time-consuming and requires costly automation and an abundance of clean water — a scarce commodity in the desert.

The self-cleaning technology was developed to overcome problems in space. The Jet Propulsion Laboratory at NASA approached the research team in 2004 because some of the landers and rovers used on Mars were solar-powered and had to contend with dirt and debris capable of blocking out light and crippling their panels and sensors.

Bursts of wind may sometimes clean the vehicles, said Rao Surampudi, a project monitor at the laboratory, which is located in Pasadena, California. "But sometimes there is no wind on Mars, and when it does come, it might deposit the dust, not remove it," he said. "Energy production is constantly cut by about 30 to 40 percent due to the dirt."

The coating developed with Mr. Mazumder and his colleagues is designed to ensure that the rovers operate at capacity consistently.

According to Mr. Mazumder, the life span of a panel should be approximately 20 years. The Mars Pathfinder, a lander launched in 1996, lasted less than a year, incapacitated by dust deposits. The panels on the Mars Spirit and Opportunity rovers, both launched in 2004, are still functioning, but are slowly becoming less proficient. (The Spirit has been put into hibernation because it has lost its mobility for other reasons.)

The new coating — a transparent, electrically sensitive material — is applied on a glass or clear plastic sheet covering the solar panel. Sensors monitor dust levels on the panel's surface, energizing the coating when dirt concentration reaches a critical level.

The charge sends a wave surging over the outside layer, which strips off approximately 90 percent of the accumulated dust and drives it to the edges of the panel. An alternating current repels both positively and negatively charged particles, imparting an electrostatic charge to those that are uncharged. The entire process is completed in less than two minutes using only a small amount of the energy generated by the panel. "It's a self-supporting system," Mr. Mazumder said.

Voytek Gutowski, who develops functional surfaces as chief research scientist at the Australian Commonwealth Scientific and Industrial Research Organization, called the self-cleaning coating "a breakthrough technology."

"And it has great potential to eliminate one of the key problems marring an effective use of solar panels," Dr. Gutowski said, "while decreasing the payback period by keeping them at their maximum possible output."

Retrofitting existing photovoltaic panels with the new technology, which has yet to be commercialized, is not expected to be complicated for existing solar manufacturers. Many of them already have access to the equipment that would allow them to transpose transparent electrodes onto solar cells.

One of the priorities for Mr. Mazumder's research team is to keep manufacturing costs below 5 percent of the total panel cost.

"We are currently developing partnerships with solar companies and are looking to bring the technology to the market as soon as possible," Mr. Mazumder said.

The electrical field technology is one of two methods for cleaning photovoltaic cells being funded by NASA. The other involves vibrating solar panels to shake debris loose, a system that necessitates fewer modifications to the panel.

"But the vibration technology is incapable of removing as many fine particles," said Mr. Surampudi, who oversaw research into both techniques. "We are still evaluating which will prove more practical for space missions."

And these systems may have applications outside of the renewable energy market. Mr. Mazumder suggested that helicopters taking off and landing in dry, dusty areas could benefit from self-cleaning windshields. The technology could also be used for lenses in laboratories and for telescopes.

But the solar industry stands to benefit most. The need for such technologies, Mr. Mazumder said, is steadily increasing with the expansion of the solar-panel market, which has reached about $24 billion. The European Photovoltaic Industry Association's latest Global Market Outlook found that growth had averaged 40 percent per year since 2000.

"When we first began our research, solar cells were considered impractical and quite expensive," Mr. Mazumder said. "Now they appear to be the only way to go."

Geothermal Energy Grows in Kenya

BY AMY YEE | FEB. 23, 2018

HELL'S GATE NATIONAL PARK, KENYA — Verdant hills stretch into the distance at Hell's Gate National Park, where zebras, buffalos, antelopes, baboons and other wildlife roam an idyllic landscape of forests, gorges and grassy volcanoes near the shores of Lake Naivasha.

Snaking over the same landscape are pipes. Miles and miles of pipes — some high enough off the ground that trucks can pass underneath and giraffes won't hit their heads — carry steam from beneath this volcanic valley to big power plants inside the park.

The valley's animal herders have long known the unusual properties of the ground under their feet. On chilly days, they warmed themselves near vents that emit plumes of hot steam. Now, Kenya is increasingly harnessing that steam to turn generators that can allow it to expand electrical service and power its rapidly growing economy.

The park, about 50 miles from the capital of Nairobi, sits over the East African Rift, a huge fracture in the earth's crust that also cuts through Tanzania, Uganda, Ethiopia and other countries. Steam from here helped generate 47 percent of Kenya's electricity in 2015, with hydropower (nearly 35 percent) generating much of the rest.

Kenya has pushed hard to harness its geothermal capabilities. It generated 45 megawatts of power with geothermal energy in 1985 and now generates about 630 megawatts; nearly 400 megawatts of that production has come online since 2014.

"No matter how you cut it, that is a significant amount of generation in the geothermal world," said Gene Suemnicht, chief executive of EGS, a California-based geothermal consultancy that has worked in Kenya.

That explosive growth has made geothermal power a promising source of renewable energy for a country of 44 million people that is expected to nearly double in population by 2050.

Much of Kenya lacks electricity; only 40 percent of its population has access to reliable service. Much of the African continent has even less: Only about 25 percent of Africans have access to reliable electricity. Although Africa is home to 16 percent of the world's population, it consumes only 3.3 percent of global power production.

Reliable energy is a vital driver of economic growth. At Oserian, one of Kenya's largest flower exporters based near Lake Naivasha, geothermal steam warms greenhouses and generates electricity at its two power plants.

Geothermal heating allows the company to sell 380 million flower stems each year and also grow "varieties of roses that would not be economically viable without 24-hour heating," said Neil Hellings, managing director of Oserian. Savings from using geothermal energy versus conventional electricity lets Oserian pay its employees more than double that of many competitors, Mr. Hellings added.

Another geothermal field already under development north of Hell's Gate was expected to bring power to 500,000 households and 300,000 small and medium-size businesses, according to the African Development Bank Group.

Other countries have used geothermal power to drive their economies. In the 1970s, geothermal development helped propel Iceland from poverty to a wealthy island nation.

The rise of Kenya's geothermal industry — it ranks ninth in the world in geothermal energy production, according to the Geothermal Council Resource, an American industry association — has helped reduce electricity rates and expand access to electricity. The government has set an ambitious goal of universal access by 2020 — but many challenges make that a very high bar to reach.

Electrical transmission and distribution — and connecting customers who can pay for service — is crucial to a viable power business. In Kenya "the grid to transport the generated power to citizens also needs substantial investment," said Victoria Cuming, head of policy at Bloomberg New Energy Finance.

Big efforts to expand Kenya's grid are underway, with about 1,500 miles of new electrical lines under construction and 3,600 miles in the works by Kenya Electricity Transmission Company, or Ketraco. The main hurdle for grid expansion will be financing. "Kenya has typically relied on concessional investors or government funding," Ms. Cuming said.

Sanjay Chandra, director of new energy development at ICF, a consultancy in the United States, noted that connecting homes or smaller businesses in the "last mile is always challenging." This is especially so in poor areas where people may not be able to afford electricity or don't use much, therefore making it relatively expensive — and financially unviable — for companies to connect them.

In western Kenya "the electrification rate is hovering around 5 percent even though 84 percent of unconnected households are within 200 meters of a connection point," Mr. Chandra said.

Last year, Kenya's demand for electricity exceeded 1,600 megawatts for the first time. Under ideal circumstances, the country has the potential to generate more than 10,000 megawatts of geothermal energy, according to Kenya Electricity Generating Company, or KenGen, which generates the majority of the country's electricity.

Across all of East Africa, there's potential for some 20,000 megawatts of geothermal energy, according to a report from agencies including the Infrastructure Consortium for Africa and the United Nations Environment Program.

But Kenya and the surrounding region face many challenges to harnessing its full geothermal potential. Lack of funding and technical expertise, poor governance, and corruption often hobble big infrastructure projects in developing countries.

And though geothermal is considered renewable energy, it does have pitfalls. While the Earth will most likely supply heat for millions of years, the underground water necessary to produce steam can be depleted if not recharged.

Yet from a geological perspective, Kenya's geothermal conditions are ideal.

"The amount of volcanism is amazing," Mr. Suemnicht said. "It's in the center of the action."

The East African Rift is one of the world's largest rift valleys, about 3,700 miles in length and 30 to 40 miles across. It is slowly splitting the African continent apart at the rate of several millimeters each year.

"Rift settings have very high potential for geothermal," Mr. Suemnicht said. "Most geothermal development occurs in tectonically active areas on Earth."

Kenya is by far Africa's geothermal leader, but nations such as Tanzania, Uganda, Rwanda, Djibouti, Eritrea and Comoros have done preliminary exploration and Ethiopia generates about 7 megawatts of geothermal power.

Tapping geothermal energy is a long and expensive process that requires special expertise. From start to finish, it can take years from site-scouting to construction to connection to actually generating electricity — and revenue.

To find suitable spots for drilling steam wells, scientists do geological, geochemical and geophysical surveillance, a process that can take three months, said Xavier Musouye, a geologist with KenGen. When suitable spots are found and assessed, drilling begins using the kind of tall rigs commonly seen at oil wells. Except for periodic maintenance breaks, these drills pound into the earth 24 hours a day for nearly two months.

At a new well site in Hell's Gate, the noise was deafening as gargantuan machinery pummeled the ground. The well will eventually reach a depth of almost two miles, joining the nearly 300 others already in place in the park.

It can cost about $6 million for a single well, and even with all the planning and testing there is still a risk of drilling an empty well. Two geothermal wells were explored in neighboring Rwanda but were unsuccessful, noted Dr. Meseret Zemedkun, energy program manager for the United Nations Environment Program.

Although it is a time-consuming process, there have been advancements to speed things along. KenGen recently started using a new kind of small power plant directly on the well head that can get up and running more quickly. These generate 7.5 megawatts compared with the large power stations that each generate 45, 105 and 140 megawatts.

Kenya, the first African country to tap geothermal power, began its programs in the late 1970s and early 1980s through funding primarily from the World Bank and guidance from the United Nations Development Program. But funders pulled out in the early 1990s amid government instability before returning toward the end of that decade.

The growth since then has been dramatic, and continues. KenGen is in the process of building a new 140-megawatt plant, financed by a $400 million loan from JICA, Japan's development agency, that is expected to start running by 2018.

Although geothermal power has led to rapid expansion of electrical service here, there are environmental trade-offs. There is the conundrum of drilling in Hell's Gate, a 26-square-mile area that is one of the country's smaller parks but has been designated a Unesco world heritage site. Some environmentalists are critical of extracting geothermal energy here. They complain that pipes and power plants are environmentally disruptive and an eyesore.

Elizabeth Mwangi-Gachau, chief environmental officer for KenGen, said the company conducts environmental assessments and tries to mitigate impact. It considers wildlife migration and behavior in its development plans. Ms. Mwangi-Gachau added that KenGen has refrained from drilling in parts of Hell's Gate that would compromise the flora and fauna, even where there is major geothermal potential.

Ms. Zemedkun of U.N.E.P. pointed out that environmentally friendly geothermal projects have been developed around the world — even within national park areas, including in the United States, Italy, Iceland, New Zealand and Japan.

At Hell's Gate, the otherworldly network of geothermal pipes can be an attraction for some tourists. KenGen has even opened a geothermal spa, following the lead of an Icelandic power company that opened the Blue Lagoon spa, a signature attraction that uses water harnessed by a nearby geothermal power plant to warm its pools.

On a sunny afternoon, groups of Kenyans basked in the spa's azure water. They weren't fazed by the sight of steel pipes at a nearby geothermal wellhead. Overhead, odorless white steam floated into the air to mingle with the clouds streaking the Kenyan sky.

Airlines Fly the Skies on a Sugar High

BY AMY YEE | OCT. 7, 2014

THE RED-AND-WHITE Boeing 737 looked like any other plane on the tarmac at Orlando International Airport. But on a clear day last July, the plane became the first commercial flight powered by a new jet fuel made from sugar cane.

The passenger flight, operated by the Brazilian low-fare airline GOL, flew from Florida to São Paulo, Brazil, on a 10 percent blend of a clear liquid called farnesane mixed with regular jet fuel.

This summer, farnesane became the third kind of renewable aviation fuel to earn approval from the standards agency ASTM International, in addition to the ones made from algae and oil seeds approved in recent years.

More commercial airlines are considering using farnesane on limited flights, said John Melo, chief executive of Amyris, the biotech firm based in California that developed farnesane in a joint venture with Total, the French energy giant.

In September, the German airline Lufthansa flew a passenger plane from Frankfurt to Berlin on farnesane, which can be mixed directly with petroleum jet fuel at a 10 percent blend without any changes to planes, engines or fueling equipment.

Renewable bio-jet fuels like farnesane hold the elusive promise of better energy security, reduced carbon emissions and lower fuel costs — an increasingly pressing concern as international regulators prepare to tighten regulations.

The global aviation industry has also set ambitious goals to reduce its greenhouse gas emissions, including slashing emissions by 50 percent by 2050 compared with 2005.

To achieve these targets, renewable fuels could be one part of the puzzle. Farnesane can reduce greenhouse gas emissions by up to 80 percent compared with petroleum fuels, when compared unmixed to petroleum fuels on a one-to-one basis, according to Amyris. Renewable fuels like farnesane "would help reduce the carbon footprint of commercial aviation," the Federal Aviation Administration said.

However, there are significant hurdles to making bio-jet fuels mainstream, namely their high cost and barriers to mass production.

They also present concerns about displacing food crops for fuel crops and razing forests. Bio-jet fuels are "not a silver bullet," said Ben Schreiber, climate and energy program director at Friends of the Earth, an environmental group. "They quickly become a negative if you try to overproduce."

Airlines like United, KLM and Alaska Airlines have flown planes powered by oil made from algae, used vegetable cooking oil and plants like camelina and jatropha. But in spite of initial excitement, commercial airlines have not widely adopted bio-jet fuels, mainly because of their high cost.

But farnesane could be more commercially viable because it is produced in an Amyris-owned factory in Brazil, which has a robust policy and infrastructure to promote and produce biofuels.

The Amyris plant in São Paulo state has a production capacity of 50 million liters a year. The company currently supplies renewable fuel to city buses in Brazil.

Brazil is the world's largest producer of sugar cane as well as the second-largest producer of ethanol. A majority of light vehicles on the roads in Brazil can run on ethanol, which is made from domestic sugar cane.

Because of its large, existing biofuel infrastructure, millions of gallons of farnesane could be produced in Brazil, Mr. Melo said. Distribution is also not a barrier. Farnesane can be easily distributed to airlines for refueling, he said.

Daniel Rutherford, program manager at the International Council on Clean Transportation, noted that when assessing a biofuel's overall environmental benefits, "what really matters is how the fuel is produced." He added that Brazil's sugar cane industry was highly productive and not very fossil fuel-intensive. However, the best way to "avoid the food versus fuel trade-off" would be to produce bio-jet fuels from waste like corn husks and tree bark through technology that is still being developed, he said.

Amyris has been developing the technology behind farnesane for more than eight years with initial funding from venture capital and private equity firms. In the last few years, the company received grants totaling about $10 million from the United States Energy Department to further develop fermentation technology.

Farnesane is made through a fermentation process in which Amyris's engineered yeast consumes sugar cane syrup to produce a hydrocarbon called farnesene. Through hydrogenation, hydrogen atoms are added to convert farnesene into a molecule called farnesane, which makes up the renewable jet fuel. Mr. Melo noted that Amyris was working on technology that could produce farnesane from other sources like organic waste.

With farnesane, "there is nothing from a technical or aviation industry standpoint holding it back," said Steve Csonka, executive director of the Commercial Aviation Alternative Fuels Initiative, a coalition of airline industry-related companies, researchers and government agencies.

According to rigorous testing by plane makers like Boeing, farnesane and other types of approved bio-jet fuel actually perform better than conventional jet fuel.

They also burn cleaner than conventional aviation fuel, said Julie Felgar, managing director of environmental strategy and integration for Boeing Commercial Airplanes. Because of close scrutiny, bio-jet fuels have to "perform as well as or better than regular jet fuel," she said.

This is a high bar because aviation fuel is more complex than fuel for cars and road vehicles.

But for Amyris and other bio-jet fuel makers, the biggest challenge is bringing down the cost.

The company would not disclose price per liter for farnesane, but Mr. Melo claimed it could match that of conventional jet fuel within two to three years. Amyris said it hoped the American government would drop protectionist policies that could hinder the sugar-based fuel in the United States.

If farnesane's price drops, the bio-jet fuel could become mainstream for airlines, Mr. Melo said. "The choice won't be, 'Do I choose renewable or not?' " he said. "The choice will be, 'Do I choose a better product or not?' "

Canada Produces Strain of Algae for Fuel

BY HILLARY BRENHOUSE | SEPT. 29, 2010

MONTREAL — The sizable scientific team at Ocean Nutrition Canada in Halifax, Nova Scotia, the world's largest supplier of omega-3 EPA and DHA fatty acid supplements, was hardly looking for an alternative to conventional fossil fuels.

In 2005, as part of a five-year research effort, the company was screening algae samples, taken from marine environments across the Atlantic provinces of Canada, for specific nutraceutical ingredients. That is when, in one of hundreds of filmy, green test tubes and flasks, it uncovered a single-celled microorganism that produces substantial quantities of triacylglycerol oil — a base for biofuel.

"It was like finding a needle in a haystack," said Ian Lucas, Ocean Nutrition Canada's executive vice president of innovation and strategy. "We got extremely lucky. This certainly isn't our core business, but we've been told by experts that this is the most efficient organism for the production of oil identified in the world to date."

Dozens of companies and academic laboratories are pursuing the objective Ocean Nutrition Canada did not know it had — to cultivate algae, the foundation of the marine food chain, as a source of green energy.

But Ocean Nutrition Canada's prolific grower, experts say, appears capable of producing oil at a rate 60 times greater than other types of algae being used for the generation of biofuels.

In view of its discovery, the company will lead a four-year consortium, formed over the past months and funded by the federal not-for-profit foundation Sustainable Development Technology Canada, to develop its proprietary organism into a commercial-scale producer of biofuels.

Canada, with its long harsh winter and short summer, would hardly seem to be the ideal place to breed algae for biofuel.

"Canada doesn't seem like the best place to be growing algae, but Canadian expertise can be applied to programs all over the world," said Dr. John Cullen of Dalhousie University's Oceanography Department in Halifax. Indeed, recent federal investments have placed Canada among the pioneering nations housing publicly funded research programs aimed at the sustainable production of energy from algae biomass.

And Canada's severe environment could actually turn out to be an advantage. It is widely recognized that growing algae might more easily be done in an equatorial region where the temperature is consistently warm and daylight varies little from 12 hours a day.

"But there is no reason not to develop the technologies in a northern climate and deploy them more equatorially," said Stephen O'Leary, a research officer at the National Research Council of Canada's Institute for Marine Biosciences, also based in Halifax.

Capable of converting sunlight and carbon dioxide into lipids and oils, photosynthetic algae can typically generate 10 to 20 times more fuel per acre than agricultural commodities like corn, used to make ethanol.

Moreover, algae do not require arable land and so need not compete with food crops for growth space. And as voracious consumers of carbon dioxide, photosynthetic algae have the potential to abate greenhouse gas emissions.

Interest in the field of algal biofuels is escalating both in Canada's public and private sectors.

The consortium, led by Ocean Nutrition, "is finally publicizing the fact that Canada has been doing a lot of work in this space for some time and is almost at the leadership position," said Rick Whittaker, vice president, investments and chief technology officer at Sustainable Development Technology Canada. The project has attracted multinational partners, including the military contractor Lockheed Martin and UOP, a unit of Honeywell that supplies technologies to the petroleum industry and is here focused on converting the algal oil into an alterative jet fuel.

"It's a big deal for Eastern Canada and a big deal for the country in general," Mr. Whittaker said. "Because of this particular algae strain and our ability to process it, this can reach a global scale."

Ocean Nutrition is now capable of growing meaningful amounts of the strain — named ONC T18 B — and keeps a stockpile in cryogenic reserve. One of the species's draws is that it produces oil by converting reduced organic compounds, not by conventional photosynthesis. Direct sunlight is not always easy to come by in Canada, and heating indoor ponds could end up consuming more energy than it produces.

"Growing algae on a pond in Canada means that it's an ice hockey rink in the winter time," Mr. Whittaker said. "We're interested in producing these things all year round without an issue."

The National Research Council's Institute for Marine Biosciences is contributing expertise as a member of the consortium. "Our role in the project is to help ONC push the biology of their organism so that it becomes the fastest-growing, best oil-producing organism it can be," Dr. O'Leary said. The aim, he said, is to enhance the physical conditions under which the algae grow.

Meanwhile, the biosciences institute is involved in its own algal biofuels initiative, encompassed by the National Bioproducts Program, a joint venture with Agriculture and Agrifood Canada and Natural Resources Canada. Begun in 2008 — though researchers at the biosciences institute have been working on algal biotechnology for more than half a century — the project's aim is photosynthetic fuel production on a large scale, mostly from algae growing in eastern Canada. A 15,000-liter, or 4,000-gallon, cultivation pilot plant at the NRC's Marine Research Station in Ketch Harbor, outside Halifax, celebrated its grand opening in June.

One of the initiative's distinguishing features is its focus on collecting local strains of algae from specific Canadian and American sites. Organisms that are indigenous and therefore acclimatized to an area naturally lend themselves to cultivation there. And this approach mitigates the risk of importing foreign species that might upset the environmental balance if unintentionally released.

"A strategy in this type of research has been to go to already established algal libraries and withdraw species known to be fast growers and good lipid producers with little consideration for where in the world they were isolated," Dr. O'Leary said. "There hasn't been enough focus on developing native strains for native deployment."

In assessing how best to grow algae for biofuel, NRC has joined forces with the U.S. Department of Energy in a collaboration formed under the auspices of the U.S.-Canada Clean Energy Dialogue. It has also teamed up with the U.S. National Renewable Energy Laboratory in Colorado and Sandia National Laboratories in New Mexico.

Other partners include a number of Canadian companies that have recently entered the algal biofuels arena, like Carbon2Algae Solutions, which ultimately plans to operate algae photobioreactors that will capture carbon dioxide from facilities like the oil sands in Alberta and use it to help local algae strains thrive.

At the biosciences institute, more than 100 species of algae have been collected and studied; about 40 of these have been brought into cultivation.

Dr. O'Leary estimates that commercialization — producing large volumes of fuel from algae to feed into Canada's network of distribution pipelines — is at least a decade away. But locating an algal cultivation facility at a source of industrial carbon dioxide, to produce biomass for local use, could be commercially viable within five years, he says.

As for Canada's advantage in this technological race, Mr. Whittaker says the ideal algae strain would be one that consumes a cheap feedstock, produces high levels of oil and is robust. Algae will grow even in the most uninviting of environments, and the harsh Canadian climate produces rugged plants.

"The thing that would suggest that Canada is at a disadvantage," Mr. Whittaker said, "is actually the advantage that allows all this to happen."

Or, as Dr. O'Leary put it: "If it'll work here, it'll work anywhere."

No Furnaces but Heat Aplenty in 'Passive Houses'

BY ELISABETH ROSENTHAL | DEC. 26, 2008

DARMSTADT, GERMANY — From the outside, there is nothing unusual about the stylish new gray and orange row houses in the Kranichstein District, with wreaths on the doors and Christmas lights twinkling through a freezing drizzle. But these houses are part of a revolution in building design: There are no drafts, no cold tile floors, no snuggling under blankets until the furnace kicks in. There is, in fact, no furnace.

In Berthold Kaufmann's home, there is, to be fair, one radiator for emergency backup in the living room — but it is not in use. Even on the coldest nights in central Germany, Mr. Kaufmann's new "passive house" and others of this design get all the heat and hot water they need from the amount of energy that would be needed to run a hair dryer.

"You don't think about temperature — the house just adjusts," said Mr. Kaufmann, watching his 2-year-old daughter, dressed in a T-shirt, tuck into her sausage in the spacious living room, whose glass doors open to a patio. His new home uses about one-twentieth the heating energy of his parents' home of roughly the same size, he said.

Architects in many countries, in attempts to meet new energy efficiency standards like the Leadership in Energy and Environmental Design standard in the United States, are designing homes with better insulation and high-efficiency appliances, as well as tapping into alternative sources of power, like solar panels and wind turbines.

The concept of the passive house, pioneered in this city of 140,000 outside Frankfurt, approaches the challenge from a different angle. Using ultrathick insulation and complex doors and windows, the architect engineers a home encased in an airtight shell, so that barely any heat escapes and barely any cold seeps in. That means a passive house can be warmed not only by the sun, but also by the heat from appliances and even from occupants' bodies.

And in Germany, passive houses cost only about 5 to 7 percent more to build than conventional houses.

Decades ago, attempts at creating sealed solar-heated homes failed, because of stagnant air and mold. But new passive houses use an ingenious central ventilation system. The warm air going out passes side by side with clean, cold air coming in, exchanging heat with 90 percent efficiency.

"The myth before was that to be warm you had to have heating. Our goal is to create a warm house without energy demand," said Wolfgang Hasper, an engineer at the Passivhaus Institut in Darmstadt. "This is not about wearing thick pullovers, turning the thermostat down and putting up with drafts. It's about being comfortable with less energy input, and we do this by recycling heating."

There are now an estimated 15,000 passive houses around the world, the vast majority built in the past few years in German-speaking countries or Scandinavia.

The first passive home was built here in 1991 by Wolfgang Feist, a local physicist, but diffusion of the idea was slowed by language. The courses and literature were mostly in German, and even now the components are mass-produced only in this part of the world.

The industry is thriving in Germany, however — for example, schools in Frankfurt are built with the technique.

Moreover, its popularity is spreading. The European Commission is promoting passive-house building, and the European Parliament has proposed that new buildings meet passive-house standards by 2011.

The United States Army, long a presence in this part of Germany, is considering passive-house barracks.

"Awareness is skyrocketing; it's hard for us to keep up with requests," Mr. Hasper said.

Nabih Tahan, a California architect who worked in Austria for 11 years, is completing one of the first passive houses in the United States for his family in Berkeley. He heads a group of 70 Bay Area architects and engineers working to encourage wider acceptance of the standards. "This is a recipe for energy that makes sense to people," Mr. Tahan said. "Why not reuse this heat you get for free?"

Ironically, however, when California inspectors were examining the Berkeley home to determine whether it met "green" building codes (it did), he could not get credit for the heat exchanger, a device that is still uncommon in the United States. "When you think about passive-house standards, you start looking at buildings in a different way," he said.

Buildings that are certified hermetically sealed may sound suffocating. (To meet the standard, a building must pass a "blow test" showing that it loses minimal air under pressure.) In fact, passive houses have plenty of windows — though far more face south than north — and all can be opened.

Inside, a passive home does have a slightly different gestalt from conventional houses, just as an electric car drives differently from its gas-using cousin. There is a kind of spaceship-like uniformity of air and temperature. The air from outside all goes through HEPA filters before entering the rooms. The cement floor of the basement isn't cold. The walls and the air are basically the same temperature.

Look closer and there are technical differences: When the windows are swung open, you see their layers of glass and gas, as well as the elaborate seals around the edges. A small, grated duct near the ceiling in the living room brings in clean air. In the basement there is no furnace, but instead what looks like a giant Styrofoam cooler, containing the heat exchanger.

Passive houses need no human tinkering, but most architects put in a switch with three settings, which can be turned down for vacations, or up to circulate air for a party (though you can also just open the windows). "We've found it's very important to people that they feel they can influence the system," Mr. Hasper said.

The houses may be too radical for those who treasure an experience like drinking hot chocolate in a cold kitchen. But not for others. "I grew up in a great old house that was always 10 degrees too cold, so

I knew I wanted to make something different," said Georg W. Zielke, who built his first passive house here, for his family, in 2003 and now designs no other kinds of buildings.

In Germany the added construction costs of passive houses are modest and, because of their growing popularity and an ever larger array of attractive off-the-shelf components, are shrinking.

But the sophisticated windows and heat-exchange ventilation systems needed to make passive houses work properly are not readily available in the United States. So the construction of passive houses in the United States, at least initially, is likely to entail a higher price differential.

Moreover, the kinds of home construction popular in the United States are more difficult to adapt to the standard: Residential buildings tend not to have built-in ventilation systems of any kind, and sliding windows are hard to seal.

Dr. Feist's original passive house — a boxy white building with four apartments — looks like the science project that it was intended to be. But new passive houses come in many shapes and styles. The Passivhaus Institut, which he founded a decade ago, continues to conduct research, teaches architects and tests homes to make sure they meet standards. It now has affiliates in Britain and the United States.

Still, there are challenges to broader adoption even in Europe.

Because a successful passive house requires the interplay of the building, the sun and the climate, architects need to be careful about site selection. Passive-house heating might not work in a shady valley in Switzerland, or on an urban street with no south-facing wall. Researchers are looking into whether the concept will work in warmer climates — where a heat exchanger could be used in reverse, to keep cool air in and warm air out.

And those who want passive-house mansions may be disappointed. Compact shapes are simpler to seal, while sprawling homes are difficult to insulate and heat.

Most passive houses allow about 500 square feet per person, a comfortable though not expansive living space. Mr. Hasper said people who wanted thousands of square feet per person should look for another design.

"Anyone who feels they need that much space to live," he said, "well, that's a different discussion."

Vast Potential in the Discomfort of Howling Winds

BY LOUISE LOFTUS | SEPT. 29, 2010

GLASGOW, SCOTLAND — The Scots have a word for their country's peculiar brand of weather: "Dreich" evokes the gray skies, driving rain and howling winds that batter the rugged northern coast of Britain.

This weather is not comfortable, but since a report in May that assessed Britain's offshore renewable energy potential, a consensus is growing about the bracing economic opportunities that it can offer to Britain, and to Scotland in particular.

The study was carried out by the energy advisory firm Boston Consulting for the Offshore Valuation Group, a coalition of government and industry organizations. The report found that the total practical offshore renewable energy generating capacity of Britain could be as much as 531 gigawatts.

Fully exploited, this capacity could, in theory, supply enough power to meet more than six times Britain's current demand for electricity. Using only a third of the potential wind, wave and tidal power resources could generate the electricity equivalent of one billion barrels of oil a year — the current British output of North Sea oil and natural gas.

If harnessed correctly that could be enough to make Britain a net exporter of electricity by 2050 and create thousands of jobs in the process. "We find ourselves in a comparable position to that of the nascent oil and gas companies in the 1970s," the report said.

About 7 percent of potential offshore energy resources are around the Welsh coast, 39 percent are off the coast of Scotland, and the remaining 54 percent are around the English coast.

The share in Scotland is the equivalent of 206 gigawatts. According to the Scottish government, harnessing about a third of that, or 68 gigawatts, could translate into power sales worth an estimated net

£14 billion, or $22 billion, by 2050. That would be equivalent to £2,700 per person in Scotland, significantly more than the £400 net per capita value in England, or the £1,000 per person value in Wales.

But tapping into that potential income stream may be problematic, for reasons that include the likelihood of shortages of skill and technology. Britain risks seeing its exploitation of offshore energy opportunities hobbled by a lack of the skilled workers needed and a lack of transmission infrastructure required to transport power from some of the remotest parts of the country to the main centers of population and industry.

The Offshore Valuation study sets out three scenarios for the next 40 years, with the most ambitious suggesting that an average of 13.1 gigawatts of wind, wave or tidal energy could be installed each year until 2050.

"Predicting up to 2050, we had to make judgments on many things," said Tim Helweg-Larsen, chairman of the Offshore Valuation Group and director of the Public Interest Research Center, an independent research institution that studies the connections between climate, energy and economics. "But all the technologies we have included are already in use or viable," he added during an interview.

The best-case scenario sees offshore wind and marine energy farms with an installed capacity to produce the energy equivalent of 2.6 billion barrels of oil a year by 2050 — more than double the output from British North Sea oil fields in 1999, their peak year of production.

These numbers take into account limitations like environmental concerns and the need to avoid shipping hazards, Mr. Helweg-Larsen said. "Without those variables, the numbers would be even bigger than they are," he added.

Meanwhile, Britain's existing electricity generating plants are aging. By 2030, 80 percent will need to be replaced, with 8.5 gigawatts of coal power capacity closing by 2017 and nine gigawatts of nuclear power capacity due to disappear as aging reactors are permanently decommissioned.

Next-generation nuclear power plants are unlikely to be ready before 2020, while clean coal technology is still regarded as commercially unviable. A new generation of gas-fired power plants could increase consumer bills by more than 60 percent, the Scottish government energy regulator said.

The hope is that the results of the Offshore Valuation Study will "wake up the right people" to a resource that already exists, can be profitable and will never run out, Mr. Helweg-Larsen said. "What the report does is to put the question back to government," he said. "The resources are there. What is the scale of your ambition?"

The Scottish minister for enterprise, energy and tourism, Jim Mather, thinks that government should step in to meet initial costs. "Capital is needed," he said, "if we put up the initial grants, then these will help attract further private investment."

"We have to make sure to get all of our ducks in a row," Mr. Mather said. "The lasting legacy of oil and gas in Scotland will be a skilled work force that can usher in these new technologies."

Renewables UK, an industry trade body, says that about 5,000 people are employed directly in British large-scale onshore and offshore wind industries. But over the next 11 years, it says, the wind energy industry alone could need as many as 60,000 recruits.

"A substantial work force is needed in the offshore wind sector to build and maintain the offshore wind farms currently planned or under construction," the industry body said in a recent report.

Preliminary results of a study financed by the European Union, and conducted by the Power cluster partnership, a cooperative network that aims to foster offshore wind development, found that skill shortages, training and industry standards need to be urgently addressed if Britain is to harness its potential.

The Power cluster study evaluates the transfer of oil and natural gas skills and standards into the renewable energy sector.

Morag McCorkindale, chief operating officer of the Aberdeen Renewable Energy Group, a public-private partnership working to transfer existing oil and natural gas expertise into offshore renewables, said the study indicated a clear need for concerted action.

"The U.K.'s deep-rooted expertise puts it at a considerable advantage to harness the renewables market because it has the infrastructure, transferable skills, research and development and all-important know-how," Ms. McCorkindale said. "Many oil and gas mechanisms, such as recognized codes of practice, sharing of information and supply chain management, are also transferable.

"It's vital that we capitalize on this expertise and build as effective a supply chain in renewables as we have in oil and gas," she said.

Despite its huge potential, Britain trails other countries in offshore production of renewable energy — particularly Germany, Denmark and Spain — and in manufacturing, design and supply chain jobs. But offshore wind represents only 1 percent of the worldwide wind market, with annual turbine sales of $60 billion. New development could signal a change in global demand that would stimulate large scale manufacturing investment. As the offshore wind industry gathers pace, Britain could still emerge as a manufacturing power.

Britain "has to make sure it has a role in negotiating with Europe," Mr. Helweg-Larsen said. "Getting out of this island mentality and getting a framework in place for exporting to Europe is the only way to exploit the full potential of the resources that are there."

Mr. Mather, the Scottish energy and tourism minister, also advocated a coordinated effort. "Scotland is sitting on a huge prize, and I think we have an obligation to harness it properly," he said.

That, however, may be hard to do. National Grid, the British power transmission company, has already acknowledged that its existing network is inhibiting the building of new generating plant in Scotland. It has said it is unlikely to be able to connect any new applicants in the next seven years. Recent estimates have indicated that it could cost as much as £4.7 billion by 2020 simply to improve existing transmission lines, even before looking at the cost of extending the geographical reach of the grid.

First Minister Alex Salmond of Scotland says he hopes that the opportunity for investors will prove attractive enough to overcome the hurdles. Speaking to financial industry executives in Edinburgh in June, he outlined an ambitious agenda. "Scotland has the natural resources and ambition to become the green energy powerhouse of Europe," he said, "with an estimated quarter of Europe's offshore wind and tidal energy resource and a tenth of its potential wave capacity.

"Capitalizing on the economic benefits of Scotland's vast natural resources requires massive investment in infrastructure," he added. "This offers the financial sector an attractive opportunity to make a positive contribution to our environment while securing sustainable returns."

To deliver the full potential of the available resources to Europe would require a large-scale network to connect production centers. The International Energy Association has estimated that, on current plans, about €200 billion, or $250 billion, would be needed to improve existing transmission routes in Europe.

At the end of 2009, the Union set up a working group on the European super-grid to open up the European electricity market to competition, facilitate cross-border trade and reduce the market dominance of existing national suppliers.

The hope is that competition will drive down prices, increase innovation and underpin the growth of a low carbon economy in Europe.

Clean Power That Reaps a Whirlwind

BY KEITH BRADSHER | MAY 9, 2007

HOUXINQIU, CHINA — The wind turbines rising 180 feet above this dusty village at the hilly edge of Inner Mongolia could be an environmentalist's dream: Their electricity is clean, sparing the horizon sooty clouds or global warming gases.

But the wind-power generators are also part of a growing dispute over a United Nations program that is the centerpiece of international efforts to help developing countries combat global warming.

That program, the Clean Development Mechanism, has become a kind of Robin Hood, raising billions of dollars from rich countries and transferring them to poor countries to curb the emission of global warming gases. The biggest beneficiary is no longer so poor: China, with $1.2 trillion in foreign exchange reserves, received three-fifths of the money last year. And as a result, some of the poorest countries are being left out.

Scientists increasingly worry about the emissions from developing countries, which may contribute to global environmental problems even sooner than previously expected. China is expected to pass the United States this year or next to become the world's largest emitter of global warming gases.

That draws attention to the Clean Development Mechanism, which has grown at an extraordinary pace, to $4.8 billion in transfer payments to developing countries last year from less than $100 million in 2002.

The Clean Development Mechanism raises its money through a complex market in trading pollution credits: businesses and governments in affluent regions like Europe and Japan help pay to reduce pollution in poorer countries, offsetting their own emissions. This helps advanced industrial nations stay within their Kyoto Protocol limits for emitting climate-changing gases like carbon dioxide.

Li Guohai, a peasant near Houxinqiu, has had free electricity since the wind turbines were erected and has freed up money for a steel plow.

For each ton of global warming gases that a developing country can prove it has eliminated, the secretariat of the Clean Development Mechanism, in Bonn, Germany, awards it a credit. Developing countries sold credits last year to richer nations for an average price of $10.70 each.

Its growth has come almost entirely by focusing on efficient projects in China and other fast-growing countries that spread the administrative costs over many large efforts, while poorer lands have received almost nothing. And that is why the program is becoming a battleground, pitting an unlikely coalition of bankers, traders, industrialists and environmentalists, who defend it, against economic development advocates, who warn of distortions.

According to the World Bank, China captured $3 billion of the $4.8 billion in subsidies last year for dozens of projects. Yet it accounted for less than two-fifths of the developing world's fossil fuel consumption, the main source of warming gases.

One of the projects is the wind farm here, nestled on a pine-forested hill beside a blue lake fringed by broad fields tilled into long furrows of freshly planted wheat. It is profitable even without the subsidies, and is owned by a group of Chinese companies traded on the Shanghai Stock Exchange.

But it is China's financial sophistication that has helped it soak up so much in subsidies. A vigorous cottage industry of project designers and brokers has sprung up in Shanghai — with workers translating forms into Chinese, promoting the program and taking steps to make it easy and inexpensive for Chinese companies to participate.

"There are a lot of people who know how to do it," said Tao Fuchang, the general manager and chief engineer of the Liaoning Zhangwu Jinshan Wind Power Electricity Company, which built and operates the turbines here.

Next in line are India, Brazil, Mexico and Argentina, which get most of the rest of the subsidies, along with South Korea — incongruously classified as a developing nation by the Kyoto Protocol, the 1997 pact to limit emissions that also led to the creation of the Clean Development Mechanism.

Trailing far behind are African countries. Payments totaled less than $150 million last year for all of Africa, where government officials say they have been largely left out of one of the biggest bonanzas for the developing world in many years.

"We see this problem everywhere in Africa," said Sateeaved Seebaluck, a high-ranking environment official in Mauritius, an island nation east of Africa.

Even when very poor countries are able to organize development projects, they may lack expertise and must sometimes pay out as much as half the credits in the form of fees for international consultants and credit brokers.

United Nations executives respond, with considerable support from environmentalists, bankers and corporations, that the program's primary task is to reduce the tonnage of carbon dioxide and other warming gases entering the atmosphere — regardless of where it comes from. By that measure, they say, the program is a success.

Kai-Uwe Schmidt, the Clean Development Mechanism's executive board secretary, said the organization was acutely aware of regional imbalances in global warming projects and hoped to address them. But setting up an emissions reduction project usually requires considerable investment.

"We do not see many investments flowing into Africa in the first place," he said.

Subsidies are readily available for a wide range of projects — straw-fired power plants, wind turbines, even the capture and burning of methane leaking from landfills. Though detailed procedures have been developed for projects in China and other fast-growing countries, they can easily be copied for use in other places.

But before manufacturers can obtain the subsidies, their national governments need to set up a legal framework for handling the money, which some of the poorest countries have not yet been able to do.

The projects that have produced the greatest number of credits so far involve attaching waste-gas incinerators to chemical factories that manufacture an ozone-destroying air-conditioner refrigerant, HCFC-22; these factories are found almost exclusively in the more prosperous developing countries.

Kristalina Georgieva, director of sustainable development strategy and operations at the World Bank, said the Clean Development Mechanism's secretariat could simplify its rules to help poorer nations.

Ms. Georgieva said the secretariat should also pay more attention to fostering renewable energy in very poor lands, because 1.6 billion people lack any electricity and it is crucial to choose power-generating technologies for them that will contribute as little as possible to global warming.

"How the developing countries choose to electrify will determine the fate of the earth," she said in a recent speech.

Some say the verification process is too burdensome for the poorest countries. But too much streamlining of the process could undermine

A farm family prepared its fields near a wind farm on the fringes of Inner Mongolia. Chinese financial skill has helped make the project profitable.

the confidence of investors in rich countries that the pollution credits are genuine, Ms. Georgieva acknowledged in an interview. "What you may get is eroding trust in the system," she said.

David Doniger, an environmental official in the Clinton administration who took part in many Kyoto Protocol drafting meetings in 1997 that led to the creation of the Clean Development Mechanism, said questions had been raised then about whether very poor countries would be able to obtain credits.

But the negotiators decided against any system for guaranteeing a division of credits by region, preferring one focused on reducing emissions wherever they occurred.

"Those were rejected on the grounds that you wanted to get more bang for the buck and they didn't want this to turn into another U.N. institution with a lot of emphasis on regional balance," said Mr. Doniger, who is now climate policy director at the Natural Resources Defense Council.

The wind turbine project here in Houxinqiu, an impoverished area of China, shows the pluses and minuses of the current system. It generates nearly 24 megawatts of electricity that would otherwise come from coal. China is already building enough coal-fired power plants each year to light all of Britain.

Farmers here still use mules to pull their steel-tip wooden plows and draw their aging wooden carts, the rough-hewn slats bleached white by years of sun and rain. The setting sun vanishes into a dark murk over the plains to the west, where China has been rapidly building coal-fired power plants.

Li Guohai, a local peasant riding his mule cart home with his wife on a recent evening, explained how he had received free electricity since the wind turbines were erected four years ago. He has saved enough money that he bought an all-steel plow for his mules to pull; the new plow now frees his son to finish junior high school and perhaps go to high school, Mr. Li said.

The project is narrowly profitable even without Clean Development Mechanism payments, Mr. Tao, the general manager, said. But the payments made the project more attractive and made it easier to raise money for it.

While Mr. Tao was reluctant to discuss the company's finances, Clean Development Mechanism records show that the wind farm saves the equivalent of 35,119 tons of carbon dioxide emissions a year. At $8 a credit, that is worth $281,000. Mr. Tao does not rely on that money to make the project viable, as the C.D.M. subsidies aim to do, but it helps him pay for more turbines.

"Without the Clean Development Mechanism, we'd still be profitable," Mr. Tao said. But "you need the C.D.M. for further expansion."

Indonesia Seeks to Tap Its Huge Geothermal Reserves

BY HILLARY BRENHOUSE | JULY 26, 2010

BALI, INDONESIA — The 17,500 islands of the Indonesian archipelago, perched perilously on the arc of seismic activity known as the Pacific Ring, are plagued by unpredictable and often deadly volcanic eruptions. But there is an upside to living with fire: vast reservoirs of underground water, heated by the earth's core, can be harnessed to generate electricity.

Indonesia has more than 40 percent of the world's geothermal reserves, enough to produce 28,100 megawatts over 30 years, equivalent to the power generated from burning 12 billion barrels of oil, according to revised figures released by the Energy and Mineral Resources Ministry in March.

Geothermal energy could conceivably power a significant part of this sprawling country of more than 227 million people. Currently Indonesia is turning out less than 1,200 megawatts from six geothermal fields scattered across Java, North Sumatra and North Sulawesi — a negligible percentage of its potential, putting it behind both the United States and the Philippines. But Indonesian officials have ambitious goals for geothermal generation.

President Susilo Bambang Yudhoyono has said that by 2025 he would like geothermal generating capacity to rise to 9,500 megawatts, or about 5 percent of the country's total requirements. And tapping into geothermal resources — a low-carbon, clean alternative to the oil and coal that dominate Indonesia's energy consumption — could help him realize another stated objective: to reduce greenhouse gas emissions at least 26 percent over the next decade.

To reach these goals, Indonesia will need an upsurge of foreign investment. In late April, Bali was the host of the 2010 World Geothermal Congress, which attracted technical experts, officials and investors from about 80 countries. "The Congress was a way of introducing Indonesia to the world and saying, 'We're open for business,' " said Ted Saeger, energy and natural resources officer at the U.S. Embassy in Jakarta.

The conference opened with the signing of 12 geothermal-related contracts worth about $5 billion, ushering in the second phase of a fast-track government program to develop Indonesia's power industry. This phase, estimated to cost $12 billion and scheduled for completion in 2014, calls for an increase in geothermal generating capacity to nearly 4,000 megawatts.

A month after the congress, the U.S. commerce secretary, Gary Locke, led a trade mission to Indonesia of representatives from 10 clean technology companies looking for opportunities in geothermal development, particularly in the outer islands. Addressing an American Chamber of Commerce luncheon in Jakarta, Mr. Locke spoke about the prospects. "We cannot be so concerned about the initial cost," he said. "Ultimately, the cost will go down, the technology will improve.

"The benefit to the planet, and to our health, and to the quality of life of today's people and future generations, is so critical," he added.

Yet his comments recognized a more problematic near-term reality. Technical risks, lengthy lead times and soaring exploration costs have deterred foreign investors seeking a quick return. Geothermal plants use wells to tap subterranean pockets of heated water, releasing pressurized steam capable of turning huge turbines. Operational and maintenance expenses are relatively low, but the initial investment in heat-extraction and power-generating technology is capital intensive, and additional infrastructure spending is often needed, for example to build access roads in remote and mountainous regions. By most estimates, moreover, preliminary geological surveys and exploratory drilling for a single plant can take seven to eight years.

"You might put $20 to $40 million into digging holes just to find out what the capacity of your field is," said Brett King of the law firm Paul, Hastings, Janofsky & Walker, in Hong Kong, which has been involved in several geothermal deals. "No one will sign contracts until you know for sure."

During the 1990s, under former President Suharto, a dozen or so companies, local and foreign, began to develop geothermal power in partnership with PLN, the national power utility. But most of these projects collapsed under the weight of the 1997 Asian financial crisis, and were canceled by Jakarta under pressure from the International Monetary Fund. Others were taken over by the government or renegotiated at lower prices, while a handful of cases went to arbitration.

In the aftermath of that experience, the Indonesian government is no longer offering sovereign guarantees to honor power purchase agreements, and international investors have been slow to return.

Regulatory and policy obstacles continue to plague the potentially lucrative sector. Investors are pushing the government to make long-term policy changes, particularly to its subsidy structure for fossil fuels. A low electricity tariff has also hampered progress, despite an average 10 percent rise this month.

"Over the last year there has been a lot of policy movement to get the investment climate in shape for foreigners to come in," Mr. Saeger, the U.S. Embassy official, said. "But key barriers remain," he added, including "a confusing tendering process and land acquisition problems."

Chevron, the U.S. energy giant that is the largest geothermal power producer in the world, has operated two geothermal fields in West Java, Salak and Darajat, since the mid-1980s. It says it intends to double its geothermal generating capacity in Southeast Asia by 2020 and is considering several of the 256 sites that Indonesia has identified as having potential. But it also says it is able to develop geothermal resources largely because it operates on contracts signed during Mr. Suharto's presidency.

Speaking at the Bali conference, James Blackwell, Chevron's head of exploration and production in the Asia-Pacific region, held up the Philippines, the world's second-largest geothermal producer, as an example to follow. Manila recently enacted a renewable energy law to stimulate private investment that he described as encouraging open and competitive power generation while reducing excessive royalties and taxes.

To encourage investment, the World Bank's Clean Technology Fund made available $400 million of financing in March, as part of an effort to bolster spending to combat climate change in the developing world and to help double Indonesia's geothermal capacity. The Indonesian government recognizes that because of PLN's poor financial condition, the risk premium required in financing power projects tends to be prohibitive. A recently established Indonesia Infrastructure Guarantee Fund, backed by the World Bank, aims to provide political and payment risk insurance for infrastructure projects.

An exploration risk mitigation fund, specifically for geothermal, is also in the works, and already the Indonesian government is offering tax incentives to investors in renewable energies, Maryam Ayuni, director general of new energy at the Energy and Mineral Resources Ministry, said at a conference in Jakarta this month.

Mr. Saeger, of the U.S. Embassy, said, "I'm encouraged by Indonesian officials' desire to get the policy right, but we'll have to see if they can overcome the obstacles."

Tricorona, a Swedish business that specializes in trading offsets from greenhouse gas reduction projects in emerging markets, is one company looking for an answer to that question. Besides biofuels and wastewater deals, Tricorona is eyeing a 50-megawatt geothermal project in Indonesia. "Geothermal holds a lot of emission reduction potential," said Sushila Maharjan, Tricorona's director for carbon sourcing in Southeast Asia. "We have a long-term view on the market and so we're interested, regardless of barriers."

If Earth Were Powered From Space

BY **HILLARY BRENHOUSE** | OCT. 12, 2010

MONTREAL — Black holes are regions of space so massively dense and in which the force of gravity is so strong that nothing, not the slightest energy particle nor wave, can escape. But if two black holes collide and merge, says Steve MacLean, president of the Canadian Space Agency, they can eject massive jets of gas at high speed.

Space is an untapped resource, Dr. Maclean told the 21st World Energy Congress, an international gathering of about 5,000 delegates who convened in Montreal last month to address the Earth's energy needs.

"The important thing to recognize is there is more energy out there on the head of a pin than you can imagine," he said in an opening speech, "and it could power the Earth for years to come."

But Dr. Maclean told the conference, space is not important only as a potential source of energy: The exploration of space could play a major role in the search for and mapping of conventional and alternative terrestrial energy supplies.

Dr. MacLean, who himself went into orbit aboard NASA shuttles in 1992 and 2006, said space-based science could also help to clarify global climate conditions.

Physicists still have a long way to go to understand phenomena like protostellar systems, and neutron stars, in which the mass of a sun can be condensed into a diameter of 20 kilometers, or 12 miles. Yet, he said, the search for understanding could help resolve the intractable problem of energy shortages on Earth.

"The solution is out there," he said in a recent interview. "It's just a matter of understanding it."

Space agencies can also help to eradicate energy poverty in more immediate ways, by collecting and making available satellite-derived data.

Space-based observation platforms are compiling vast amounts of highly detailed data that can contribute to finding new energy sources, monitoring climate change and tracking energy use and supply.

There are now 70 satellites "considering the future of the Earth," he said, and in 10 years that number is likely to rise 300. "The type, volume and quality of data from space has vastly improved over the last two decades," he said, and data processing has made dramatic advances. "In a way you almost can't keep up with it."

James R. Drummond, a researcher at Dalhousie University's Department of Physics and Atmospheric Science in Halifax, Nova Scotia, whose work includes measuring atmospheric content from space, is equally excited about these developments.

"If you had told me when I was a young scientist in the 1970s what we would be doing in 2010, I'd have been amazed," he said. Dr. Drummond is involved with Measurement of Pollution in the Troposphere, or Mopitt, a Canadian instrument launched into orbit aboard Terra, NASA's first Earth Observing System spacecraft, in 1999.

Mopitt monitors carbon monoxide emissions and their movement, which can be used to track uncontrolled burning on the planet. This summer it was used to chart the emissions from wildfires in and around Russia, confirming that local pollution sources have global effects.

Other compounds, like carbon dioxide, and their variations over the terrestrial surface, can be followed in a similar way. Carbon monoxide measurements are more accurate, but tracking the principal greenhouse gases from space is a technique that holds promise.

"It's an area of measurement that's just beginning to be feasible," said Dr. Drummond. "It challenges our technology to the absolute limit."

Data from the primary satellite being used to trace carbon dioxide, the Greenhouse Gases Observing Satellite, or Gosat, launched by Japan last year, is just now becoming available. Ultimately, the data will help to monitor and verify compliance with international agreements and regulations on greenhouse gas emission reductions.

Monitoring the composition of the atmosphere from space complements ground monitoring, Dr. Drummond said. Terrestrial monitoring can observe how much pollution is released into the atmosphere and from where, but cannot follow the movement of trace elements. Space monitoring shows where trace elements go but can be less good at showing precisely where they come from.

Still, "the nice thing about space is that it's even-handed," Dr. Drummond said. "A single space craft in low earth orbit can make measurements over the entire globe fairly frequently."

Satellite-derived data is also being used to identify and assess potential clean energy projects.

RETScreen, an analysis software provided free by the Canadian government — and currently employed by about 265,000 users in more than 200 countries — helps individuals and institutions to detemine whether or not a proposed renewable energy, energy efficiency or cogeneration venture is viable. Its algorithms depend, in part, on scientific information being gathered by NASA. A satellite can, for instance, verify how much solar radiation is available to help establish the feasibility of introducing solar-powered water pumps in Africa.

RETScreen operates about 5,000 ground monitoring stations, but mostly these are located in industrialized countries, at airports or military bases. "When it comes to the developing world, satellites are really our only reliable source of data," said Gregory Leng, director of RETScreen International.

Mr. Leng's team has been collaborating with NASA's Langley Research Center in Virginia for more than a decade. "It was a meeting of the minds," he said. "We had the common objectives of trying to combat climate change and promote socio-economic development. Now, their climate data and our software have become the global standard in clean energy analysis."

New monitoring tools will allow RETScreen users — from small-scale farmers to major utilities — to track the performance of energy projects they have installed, using data only eight days old transmitted by NASA from its observation satellites.

Those satellites, Dr. MacLean of the Canadian Space Agency says, have a momentous role to play in the efficient use of resources.

High resolution space data help in a range of applications, from improving disaster management to deciding safe locations for offshore oil wells. "If you have a tsunami off the South Pacific that's going to happen every time there's a shift in the fault line, you're not going to put an oil rig there," Dr. MacLean said.

Images from space predicted the spread of dengue fever caused by the floods that followed the Haiti earthquake; land use data — the amount of moisture in the soil, for example — can help farmers generate higher crop yields using less energy; satellite information allows for safer navigation in uncharted waters, to gain access to untapped energy reserves. "To become fully operational, many of these things are going to require relatively minor investments considering the return we're going to get," Dr. MacLean said.

His hope is that outer space and its assets become an essential element of government infrastructure and that the data collected are used to inform energy policy. "The quality of the data that can be realized has so dramatically changed in recent years," he said. "We are now in a position to make a difference." Canada alone operates four satellites and has just received approval for three more that will be launched toward 2015. And at the beginning of this month the Canadian Space Agency held an international conference on the use of data images from Radarsat 2 — its second radar satellite, launched in 2007 — the tone of which echoed Dr. MacLean's closing remarks at the Congress: "Space can take the challenge of accessible and sustainable energy into the future."

Australia Powers Up the World's Biggest Battery — Courtesy of Elon Musk

BY ADAM BAIDAWI | NOV. 30, 2017

ADELAIDE, AUSTRALIA — The state of South Australia announced on Friday that it had powered up the world's biggest battery ahead of schedule: a feat already being heralded as one of this century's first great engineering marvels and a potential solution to the country's energy woes.

The battery is the size of an American football field. It is capable of powering 30,000 homes, and its rapid deployment reflects the union of a blackout-prone state and a flashy entrepreneur, Elon Musk, the founder of Tesla Motors, who pledged to complete its construction in 100 days or do it for free.

"This is history in the making," said Jay Weatherill, the premier of South Australia. In a statement, Tesla said the completed battery "shows that a sustainable, effective energy solution is possible."

Debate over the battery's potential has become intense. Federal lawmakers who favor fossil fuels argue that its impact is being exaggerated, while supporters gush that the state's embrace of Mr. Musk could change the future of energy in Australia — and the world.

Regardless, experts say, the moment of disruption is here.

And it all started with a tweet, read on a couch.

Mr. Weatherill, a Labor Party politician who has tried to promote his state as a magnet for innovation since taking office in 2011, was at home on his sofa in March when his phone began lighting up.

He was just days away from announcing a plan to deal with the power failures that had plagued his state for years.

On his phone came Twitter notification after Twitter notification with news that would upend his plan: Mr. Musk had offered to build the most powerful battery ever made, and do it faster than ever imagined.

Recalling that moment, Mr. Weatherill said he started to sweat. If he embraced Mr. Musk's proposal, would it look like a billionaire American entrepreneur was strong-arming his state into redefining its energy policy? Was Mr. Musk's offer real, or merely a publicity stunt?

When Mr. Musk was asked by the Australian entrepreneur (and fellow billionaire) Mike Cannon-Brookes "how serious" he was about his offer, the American mogul doubled down.

"Tesla will get the system installed and working 100 days from contract signature or it is free," Mr. Musk tweeted. "That serious enough for you?"

"Of course, the whole thing then exploded, and everyone's piling on me, saying 'Grab it!'" Mr. Weatherill said at a conference in Adelaide, the state's capital, in September.

For Mr. Weatherill, the project has been a repudiation of a federal policy that de-emphasizes renewable energy. For Mr. Musk, the battery has been a headline-grabbing venture that could prove that his radical vision of the world's energy future is both functional and economical.

"This fits into his M.O. of doing these big, grandstanding things to get attention for the company and the technology that he's building," said Ashlee Vance, the author of a 2015 biography of Mr. Musk. "Tesla's at this really critical stage where they're trying to be both a car company and an energy company at the same time."

Australia is a fitting target for Mr. Musk. The country is the world's largest exporter of coal. By most measures, it is the sunniest continent on earth. It has abundant wind and hydroelectric power capabilities. And yet the cost of electricity in Australia increased 20 percent from 2012 to 2016, and Australians this year paid between 50 and 100 percent more for their power than Americans, according to experts.

South Australia has the highest electricity prices in the world. This imbalance of supply and demand has resulted in regular blackouts and astronomical bills for the state's 1.7 million residents.

The high-capacity Tesla battery does not create energy, it just stores it. The state already invests in wind and solar energy. The battery would give it a bank of saved energy, which could ease pressure during periods of high demand and help better manage the electrical grid.

"More than 40 percent of South Australia's electricity is coming from wind, which is good," said Tony Wood, an energy director at the Grattan Institute, a think tank. "But the consideration of how to integrate it — and manage that intermittency — wasn't so good."

The day after Mr. Weatherill was roused from his couch in March, he and Mr. Musk spoke on the phone about the proposal. The Australian, knowing the tech mogul's ability to stir the news media, had one demand: If Tesla were to win the contract, Mr. Musk would appear in South Australia to announce it to the world.

"He usually doesn't come for announcements of winning a tender," Mr. Weatherill said, "but he said he'd come."

Mr. Musk nearly broke his promise, after a rocket launch by his company SpaceX was delayed. But in September, Mr. Musk arrived in Adelaide to announce the $50 million deal and to start the 100-day countdown to the project's completion.

"What this serves as is a great example to the rest of the world of what can be done," Mr. Musk said at the time, adding that half the battery had already been finished.

Mr. Musk declined to be interviewed for this article.

In March, when Mr. Musk first presented his proposal, Prime Minister Malcolm Turnbull spoke with the entrepreneur and tweeted enthusiastically about its potential.

Months later, when Tesla and the French renewables company Neoen were awarded the contract, however, Mr. Turnbull's Liberal Party government assailed the battery project and continued its attack on South Australia's energy policy.

"30,000 South Australian households could not get through watching one episode of 'Australia's Ninja Warrior' with this big battery," said Scott Morrison, the country's treasurer.

Mr. Turnbull's government has promoted fossil fuels over renewable energy to stimulate growth and prevent South Australia's power shortages. The government has questioned the battery's capacity, implied the state has been hoodwinked by a clever salesman and suggested that Mr. Weatherill was looking for publicity ahead of a 2018 election.

"The Tesla battery has been sold to the people of South Australia as an answer to their woes," Josh Frydenberg, the energy minister, wrote in an email. "But in reality it is just a fraction of the storage and backup that South Australia needs."

Franck Woitiez, the general manager of Neoen's Australia division, which will operate the battery from its wind farm, said the Turnbull government was out of touch with the future of renewable energy.

"There's no turning back," said Mr. Woitiez. "It's not tomorrow, it's now."

The next several weeks, the beginning of Australia's summer, will be crucial for judging the battery's success.

"Summer is when Australia gets its peak demand," said Mr. Wood, the energy researcher. "It will be a very important and high-profile demonstration in the role that batteries can play."

But some experts said the stakes would be even higher for Mr. Musk. He could shop the idea globally — if it works.

"He needs these battery packs to really become effective," said Mr. Vance, Musk's biographer. "He needs this to justify the entire reason of Tesla's existence."

CHAPTER 3

The Business of Clean Energy

Energy production has been part of the world's economy for centuries, and now clean energy is, too. Old methods of energy production, such as coal and natural gas, are being replaced. As methods for producing clean energy develop and become more mainstream, existing power companies hope to become part of emerging industries in order to keep their revenues healthy. In addition, companies are being founded to help produce and market clean energy on a large scale. However, new methods require new approaches, and many utilities and investors are struggling to generate profits from them.

Warren Buffett's Big Bet on Renewables in Nevada

BY FELICITY BARRINGER | OCT. 7, 2014

MOAPA, NEV. — Roads often follow rivers, taking advantage of the level ground created by water. But here in the desert of south central Nevada, the road and the river grew together. Only the river does not carry water. At the edge of Interstate 15, a crackling river of electrons provides power not just to Nevada's homes, mines and casinos, but to parts of California as well.

For years, many of those electrons were generated by coal, a fuel now largely abandoned here thanks to both economics and legislative decree. Now an increasing percentage of them are coming from

A section of the One Nevada Transmission Line near Coyote Springs, Nev.

renewable sources — geothermal, solar and wind. This makes them all the more salable now that California, the biggest energy market in the West, severely restricts the purchase of electricity associated with excessive greenhouse gases.

This has not escaped the attention of Warren E. Buffett, the country's premier investor. Through his companies, he has in recent years acquired two major utilities, NV Energy and PacifiCorp Energy, which are poised to take advantage of the energy market recently expanded by California.

Thanks in part to the transmission lines alongside Interstate 15, Mr. Buffett's company, Berkshire Hathaway, and its subsidiary Berkshire Hathaway Energy stand to make steady, predictable profits in an energy market undergoing transformations.

"This is not a value play," said Christine Tezak, managing director of research at ClearView Energy Partners, referring to Mr. Buffett's normally conservative investing approach. "He's looking at this as a way to participate in the structural shift taking place in the power and energy industry."

In the short term, the transition is going to mean construction of many renewable power plants in Nevada. Around sunbaked Las Vegas, these have been solar plants. Further north, they have been geothermal plants. They help make Nevada, a state whose energy was largely coal-fired 10 years ago, a good fit for the Environmental Protection Agency's pending rule discouraging coal-fired plants.

"The goal of the rule was to send a small market signal to the utilities of the direction they should move in," said Jared Blumenfeld, the director of E.P.A.'s Region 9, which covers the Southwest and Hawaii. Existing state mandates, he said, ensured that "in some cases they were already moving in that direction."

California's newly formed "energy imbalance market" — a multistate grid system that aims to ensure steady power despite the variable output of wind and solar — will create more customers for the new renewables as well as the considerable coal-generated energy of PacifiCorp.

Stefan Bird, a senior vice president of PacifiCorp, said the system would use power sources spread over the region to increase the grid's efficiency. "You get into different geographical regions; wind performs differently in different areas," he said. Similarly, solar plants in California not at optimal power in the morning could be offset by Nevada installations to the east already at full strength.

Regulators overseeing the market say they believe the system will save consumers money and eventually will be able to include everything from PacifiCorp's Wyoming-based wind projects to Nevada's solar and geothermal resources, ensuring that power can be dispatched in minutes to areas of unexpected demand. NV Energy expects to join the new California market in a year, after it gets federal approval.

It has taken years to assemble the pieces of the puzzle that have made these investments enticing to Mr. Buffett and others. In those years, the energy market in the Far West and Southwest has been transformed, by both the falling price of natural gas and the rise of renewables.

In 2005, Berkshire Hathaway Energy bought PacifiCorp, a Western utility now providing about 10.5 gigawatts of energy from Oregon to Wyoming, for $5.1 billion. In 2013, Mr. Buffett, who has long expressed his conviction that coal-fired energy will be a thing of the past, paid $5.6 billion for NV Energy, which has more than six gigawatts of generation capacity — more than 15 percent of it renewable power, largely solar and geothermal. Much of the rest is fired by natural gas.

One pressing early need for the new plants was finding new routes to the energy market. For decades, generating plants have been located near coal train tracks or natural gas pipelines, with power lines designed for them.

But solar, wind and geothermal energy cannot travel by train or pipeline. In Nevada, a new high-voltage line now runs more than 230 miles from Ely in the north — near the wellspring of the state's geothermal resources — to the Las Vegas area. A $343 million federal loan guarantee undergirded the $552 million project.

The inverted triangles that carry some of this line, called the One Nevada Transmission Line or ON Line, now parallel Interstate 15 near Las Vegas, along with the older, arms-outstretched towers of earlier lines. The new ON Line now has limited capacity to send power through hookups to California; it must be enhanced to send more Nevada energy south and west.

In March, a variety of stakeholders broke ground for the Moapa Southern Paiute Solar Project, designed to produce 250 megawatts of solar power to be used by the Los Angeles Department of Water and Power. A second, 200-megawatt solar plant is also planned on Moapa Paiute tribal land. That solar energy will partly make up for the Los Angeles agency's decision last year to sell its stake in the Navajo Generating Station in Arizona, divesting itself of coal-fired power to comply with California law.

NV Energy's Reid Gardner power station — not far north of Las Vegas and near the Moapa Paiute reservation — also provided coal-fired power to California. Its stored coal ash waste, reservation members believe, hurt their health. Along with the Sierra Club, they sued NV Energy; the lawsuit is pending. Aletha Tom, the chairwoman of the Moapa band, said, "I never thought of the power plant as a threat" years ago. "I never knew the danger it would do to people's health," she said. Now the solar projects will be an economic asset, she said.

This summer, the Nevada Public Utilities Commission approved a 110-megawatt solar plant in the Amargosa Valley, on the western edge of the state. A $1 billion, 250-megawatt project called Silver State South will cover nearly four square miles with solar panels near the California border.

The federal carbon reduction rule was not the only government signal pushing Nevada to abandon coal and embrace renewables. Harry Reid, the Senate majority leader, as well as the State Legislature and Gov. Brian Sandoval have pitched in. Both Mr. Reid and Mr. Sandoval supported a 2013 state law that forced the closure of the Reid Gardner coal boilers and made it easier for NV Energy to use ratepayer dollars to build new plants.

Critics see a political quid pro quo. "The intent of the legislation was clearly to reward the utility for the early closure of Reid Gardner by enabling it to replace that capacity with its own new power plants paid for by the ratepayers," said Robert D. Kahn, the executive director of the Northwest and Intermountain Power Producers Coalition, which opposed it.

NV Energy responded with a statement saying the new law required it to replace the disappearing coal-fired energy with 600 megawatts from its own resources and 300 megawatts from outside providers.

Looking at the utility's plans to build new renewable energy sources, and attempts to constrain state regulators' efforts on behalf of ratepayers, Mr. Kahn asked, "What are their economic objectives — to meet

Nevada load, or will they expect and plan on markets farther west?"

California's changing energy market makes the latter objective more attainable.

As Geoffrey Lawrence, a senior legislative analyst with the Nevada Policy Research Institute, explained, NV Energy is a more attractive investment even without an expanded market because the 2013 legislation envisions ratepayers' shouldering much of the cost of new facilities.

Plants that the ratepayers buy increase shareholder value. "They are spending more money to produce the same amount of power," Mr. Lawrence said. "And they are guaranteed an 8 to 11 percent return."

How Producing Clean Power
Turned Out to Be a Messy Business

BY DAVID GELLES | AUG. 13, 2016

On the edge of a bucolic field in Princeton, N.J., an eco-friendly office building recently opened its doors. Plants festoon the roof, a living wall is planned for the lobby, and rainwater storage tanks supply the building's needs. In the parking lot there are wind turbines, solar panels and electric vehicle charging stations.

It is the picture of a sustainable future, one in which society's insatiable demand for electricity can be met without polluting the planet.

The same cannot be said of the building's tenant, NRG Energy.

The biggest independent power producer in the country, NRG sells electricity to utilities, companies and individual homes. To generate all that wattage, it burns enormous amounts of natural gas, coal and oil, making NRG one of the country's biggest polluters.

A worker inspecting an NRG solar installation in Spencer, Mass.

It isn't trying to muck up the planet; that's just the nature of the business NRG is in. The electricity industry is the biggest source of greenhouse gas emissions in the United States, according to the Environmental Protection Agency. In 2014, NRG was the fourth-largest emitter of carbon dioxide among the country's power producers.

The business of providing Americans with electricity hasn't evolved much in a century. But today, growing concerns about climate change, affordable wind and solar power, and the potential for distributed generation are pressuring utilities and power producers like NRG to clean up their acts, and fast.

"Our industry is going though massive transformation, the likes of which we've never seen," said Mauricio Gutierrez, the recently installed chief executive of NRG. "The industry has never seen this much turnover."

All this transformation has been particularly tumultuous for NRG, which has weathered more than its share of mishaps and unintended consequences: In May, for example, a fire knocked out a crucial tower at a cutting-edge but troubled solar power plant that the company manages in the Southern California desert. Its big bets on residential solar and on a national charging network for electric vehicles were ahead of their time and fizzled.

The shale and fracking booms in the United States made natural gas cheap and abundant, pulling down the price of electricity and making power sources that NRG still depends on heavily — including coal, nuclear and renewables — less profitable. Investors lost faith in the company, NRG's stock plummeted, and its previous chief executive was summarily fired, replaced by Mr. Gutierrez.

Far from emerging as an industry pioneer, NRG has become a cautionary tale. A power-hungry nation needs to change the way it is fueled, but as NRG shows, transitioning to clean power is messy business.

"The power producers and utilities are the canaries in the coal mine," said Aron Cramer, C.E.O. of Business for Social Responsibility, a consulting firm. "And there's a lot of road kill in the midst of this transition to a lower-carbon energy system."

No two companies face the exact same set of challenges. But at some level, the quandary preoccupying NRG is one that all power producers and utilities will ultimately face: how to make more electricity while emitting fewer greenhouse gases.

NRG wasn't always a clean-energy proponent. Until recently, it was just another power producer, burning fossil fuels to electrify the grid.

In 2003, it tapped David Crane to be its chief executive. Mr. Crane, who previously ran a traditional London-based power company, set about expanding NRG's core business. He acquired Reliant Energy, which sells electricity to homes and businesses in Texas, as well as GenOn Energy, a rival based in Houston. These moves vastly expanded NRG's scale, and its emissions.

By 2006, Mr. Crane began to respond to the climate crisis and became one of the country's most unlikely environmentalists.

BRYAN ANSELM FOR THE NEW YORK TIMES

Mauricio Gutierrez on the rooftop of NRG's headquarters in Princeton, N.J.

At first, he made modest changes. NRG bought a wind power company, which it later sold. Soon, though, Mr. Crane made large investments in wind and solar plants and spent heavily on pet projects like a national network of electric-car charging stations.

Seemingly overnight, the fossil fuels executive became a champion of renewable energy. He wanted to turn the hub-and-spoke utility model — with big power plants sending electricity out to homes and businesses — inside out.

Instead, in Mr. Crane's vision, solar panels and wind turbines would blanket the country, heralding an era of distributed energy production. He called environmental protection a "moral imperative." Last year, NRG said it would slash carbon emissions in half by 2030 and reduce them by 90 percent by 2050.

"It's the destiny of NRG to be a leader," Mr. Crane said at the groundbreaking of the new headquarters, "to create a more sustainable and prosperous future while winning the fight against climate change."

Mr. Crane was channeling the spirit of the time. In December, world leaders in Paris pledged to combat climate change. The United States said it would cut its greenhouse gas emissions by more than a quarter in 10 years. With wind and solar power cheaper than ever and consumers starting to embrace energy-saving technologies, these targets could be within reach.

But the climate crisis won't be solved with more Teslas alone. If the goals set in Paris are to be met, big electricity producers like NRG will need to reduce emissions while increasing power production. So Mr. Crane set about trying to retool NRG's fleet of dirty power plants while building a new generation of utility-scale wind and solar projects.

NRG's dual personality — fossil fuel giant and clean energy pioneer — is on display at two relatively new facilities on opposite ends of the country.

Just south of Los Angeles International Airport, four smokestacks punctuate the sandy coastline. There in one form or another since the 1950s, they are part of the El Segundo Energy Center, which produces enough electricity to power nearly 450,000 homes.

At first glance, it is just another power plant burning cheap and abundant natural gas. Yet the El Segundo plant is among the most sophisticated of its kind. The two operational units, which came online in 2013, replaced inefficient relics constructed a half-century ago. Wastewater is recycled, emissions controls minimize the production of nitrogen oxide and carbon monoxide, and a mix of combustion and steam turbines greatly enhance the amount of energy derived from the gas.

And perhaps most critically, the El Segundo Energy Center is only occasionally generating power.

A generation ago, it operated almost constantly, feeding the vast energy needs of Los Angeles. But over the last several years, big power companies — including NRG — have constructed enormous solar power plants in Southern California, supplying a growing share of daytime electricity.

When the sun is shining, NRG's new high-tech gas-fired power plant is often dormant, coming alive only when demand ramps up and the sun has dimmed. In that sense, the El Segundo plant is a big leap forward. Yet the very need to pour millions of dollars into retrofitting this gas-fired plant on the picturesque shore of the Pacific Ocean shows just how much work has yet to be done.

Across the country, in Spencer, Mass., NRG is putting the final touches on a community solar project on the grounds of St. Joseph's Abbey, a Trappist monastery. There, on rolling green hills near the monks' quarters, hundreds of hard-hatted workers are busy erecting thousands of solar panels.

The electricity generated from those panels will flow through new transmission lines, which were required because the existing grid infrastructure could not handle the influx of solar energy. The project will power about 2,000 nearby homes, which should have lower and more reliable electricity bills.

By NRG's standards, the solar plant is relatively small, but more are in the works. With enough such plants on the grid, they could help NRG achieve its ambitious emissions reductions targets.

This is exactly the kind of change that Mr. Crane championed. And yet he is no NRG. He was abruptly fired in December, after NRG stock plummeted 63 percent in a year.

Earnings fell as cheap natural gas made NRG's coal-fired plants less competitive, and investors had grown weary of Mr. Crane's focus on clean energy. Even as NRG's core business was losing money, Mr. Crane devoted much of his quarterly earnings calls to discussions about clean-power projects.

"We all believe in renewables," said Shahriar Pourreza, an analyst with Guggenheim Partners. "But there was such a change in the message of the company that investors lost confidence in the management team."

The NRG board named the company's chief operating officer, Mr. Gutierrez, as the new leader. He had grown up in Mexico City, where

Computers being installed at NRG's new headquarters in Princeton, N.J.

electricity was sometimes spotty. Mr. Gutierrez joined his family's engineering company, then worked for Dynegy, a power producer in Houston, before joining NRG. Yet he says that like his predecessor, he is committed to environmental stewardship.

He drives a red Tesla and uses a Nest thermostat to remotely manage the temperature in his solar-paneled home in New Jersey. A Catholic, Mr. Gutierrez says he draws motivation from Pope Francis, who last year released "Laudato Si," an encyclical on the environment.

"When a spiritual leader like the pope calls out our moral responsibility toward the environment, it's a pretty big thing," Mr. Gutierrez said. "It transcends science and policy."

He was engaged in efforts to combat climate change well before Paris. As Mr. Crane's C.O.O., he led an NRG task force that recommended that the company adopt ambitious targets for emissions reduction. Mr. Gutierrez recently recommitted to those goals. "Renewables is something that's very important for our portfolio," he said. "It's good business."

Mr. Gutierrez has a tricky balancing act. He must appease demanding investors and a skittish board, which most likely means reining in some of Mr. Crane's clean-energy ventures. Yet he must also fill the shoes of a chief executive who had raised hopes among environmentalists that a big energy producer was getting serious about climate change. He must profitably manage gas and coal assets — which still make up most of the company's power generation, sales and profits — while also preparing for a future that is more dependent on solar and wind.

Analysts are pleased with Mr. Gutierrez's performance so far. He has simplified the corporate structure, played down some of Mr. Crane's side projects and focused on the balance sheet. NRG shares have risen 40 percent since Mr. Gutierrez took over.

"With the old management, there was such a change in message, the company started to lose credibility," Mr. Pourreza said. "Mauricio is leading this company in the right direction."

But how NRG will actually achieve vast reductions in its carbon footprint is unclear. As long as it is burning so much gas and coal, it will remain a major emitter of greenhouse gases. And while Mr. Gutierrez speaks hopefully of developments in carbon-capture technology and utility-scale battery storage, practical solutions remain elusive. "Do we have a perfect line of sight on how we're going to get there? No," he said. "Do we have a road map? Yes."

Complicating matters, the Obama administration's signature effort to reduce greenhouse gas emissions from the power sector — the Clean Power Plan — is tied up in the courts. (NRG was among the companies that petitioned the E.P.A. to modify the plan, arguing that it made the power sector too reliant on natural gas.) The ambiguous fate of that plan has added regulatory uncertainty to an industry already in flux.

"You have these goals set in Paris, you have a framework for getting there through the Clean Power Plan, and you have the judicial branch saying stop," said Ralph Izzo, chief executive of Public Service Enterprise Group, a New Jersey utility. "You can't make economic decisions in that environment."

Even NRG's big renewable projects — installations that are supposed to one day replace coal- and gas-fired plants — are mired in problems. In the Southern California desert, NRG oversees operations at Ivanpah, the world's largest solar thermal installation, where thousands of mirrors reflect the sun at enormous towers and water is converted to steam that powers turbines. NRG owns the plant along with BrightSource Energy and Alphabet, the parent company of Google.

Heralded as a beacon of clean energy when it opened in 2014, Ivanpah has been continually troubled.

From the outset, it produced less electricity than expected. Over the last few years, the cost of solar panels fell sharply, making Ivanpah's power comparatively expensive. In March, the consortium that owns the plant nearly defaulted on a contract with Pacific Gas & Electric, the Northern California utility.

Then in May, a fire at the plant knocked out one of the towers, raising new questions about the project's viability. Last week, when NRG reported quarterly earnings, it said that revenue from its renewables businesses was down 14 percent to $57 million, largely the result of problems at Ivanpah.

This isn't the first time that a big energy company has made ambitious plans to become a leader in green energy, only to be reined in. In 2000, BP introduced its "Beyond Petroleum" tagline and began investing heavily in renewable energy. It committed billions of dollars to wind and solar projects, and made investments in carbon capture and biofuels.

After a decade of investment, BP largely backed off its renewables program. Most of its money was still coming from oil and gas, and the company set about selling its solar and wind power assets. They simply weren't profitable enough.

"It's difficult to recall that 10 years ago BP was one of the darlings of the green movement," said Justin Adams, managing director of

Mike Colación, an operator, walked around transformers as he made his rounds at El Segundo Energy Center. The retrofitted NRG plant is often dormant, only occasionally generating electricity when demand ramps up and the sun goes down. It can produce enough to power nearly half a million homes in the Los Angeles area.

global lands for the Nature Conservancy and a former executive at BP working on renewables.

"Through that period, some investors were interested, most were ambivalent at best and some downright skeptical at worst," he said. "What on earth was BP doing, taking its eyes off its core business and tinkering around with renewables?"

At NRG, Mr. Gutierrez has already backed away from residential solar and electric-vehicle charging projects that Mr. Crane held so dear. So far, however, there are no signs that NRG will completely reverse course. Mr. Gutierrez is still pushing community solar power, and NRG provides solar installations to big companies like Whole Foods. Last week, NRG spent nearly $200 million to acquire more solar and wind assets.

Today, NRG generates about 9 percent of its electricity from renewable assets, up from less than 1 percent in 2008, and that figure is likely to grow. Across the industry, a majority of power plants being built today use renewables, not fossil fuels.

Mr. Crane has not gone quietly into the night. In a letter to NRG employees shortly after his ouster, he said there was "no growth in our sector outside of clean energy; only slow but irreversible contraction following the path of fixed-line telephony." Soon after that, he wrote a blog post titled "If I Was Right, Why Was I Fired?"

"The sad moral of this story is that it's very hard to be a C.E.O. for tomorrow, when the markets only care about being a C.E.O. for today," said Mr. Cramer of Business for Social Responsibility. "I don't think anyone really questions his vision, but he wasn't given any opportunity to put it into action."

Mr. Gutierrez says he shares his predecessor's vision. By 2050, he envisions enormous batteries storing solar power generated during the day, allowing people to use it at night. Distributed energy will be more common, as Mr. Crane predicted. Carbon-capture technology will make the burning of fossil fuels much less environmentally destructive, Mr. Gutierrez hopes. Perhaps coal-fired power plants will be gone altogether.

"We are a part of the problem," he said. "But we are also a big part of the solution."

It's an appealing vision of a green energy system, one that could fulfill the needs of an electricity-hungry world without spoiling the environment. But how NRG gets there — especially with investors and a board that seem intolerant of bold steps — remains vague at best. For now, Mr. Gutierrez is caught in the middle: hoping to arrive at a cleaner future while still satisfying today's investors, rolling out fields of solar while also burning tons of gas and coal.

"Let's all acknowledge that we can't change our energy system overnight," Mr. Cramer said. "But how do we start making meaningful progress? Saying 90 percent by 2050 is the easy part. We need to start making progress now."

Buying Into Solar Power,
No Roof Access Needed

BY DIANE CARDWELL | JUNE 19, 2014

LIKE MANY CONSUMERS, David Polstein had already done much to reduce energy use in his large Victorian home in Newton, Mass. He replaced his appliances with energy-efficient models, installed better heating and put in new insulation. But he was unable to get a solar system to reduce his utility bill, he said, because his roof is too small and shady to make it worthwhile.

Now, that could be changing. Mr. Polstein is considering joining a so-called community solar garden that is under development in his part of the state, one of many similar new arrangements now available in Massachusetts. Through the approach — largely pioneered in Colorado and spreading across the country — customers buy into a solar array constructed elsewhere and receive credit on their electricity bills for the power their panels produce.

For developers, such shared or community solar arrays create a new market from the estimated 85 percent of residential customers who can neither own nor lease systems because their roofs are physically unsuitable for solar or because they do not control them — like renters and people living in large apartment buildings. And for those customers, it offers a way into the solar boom, whether they seek to contribute to the spread of clean energy or to reap the potential cost savings.

"I pretty much realize that if I'm going to do this sort of thing," Mr. Polstein, a violin maker, said, "this is the only way I'm going to be able to do it."

Massachusetts passed its law enabling community renewable energy projects in 2008 and saw at least one town solar garden begin operating in Brewster in 2012. Now, Clean Energy Collective, a leading developer, is building systems that are due to start producing power in Massachusetts by the end of this month. The company has teamed with Next Step Living of Boston, a home energy-efficiency company, which is selling the product to consumers across Massachusetts.

Several other places, including California, Minnesota and Washington, D.C., have laws to establish their programs, while others have proposals at some stage of drafting. In New York, for instance, a bill is working its way through the State Legislature.

"There's no ability to really put solar on your roof when you live in an apartment — you just don't own the roof," said Amy Paulin, an assemblywoman representing Westchester.

Ms. Paulin, who is chairwoman of the Energy Committee, co-sponsored the bill after learning of the concept from advocates including Vote Solar, a group that promotes solar energy. Encouraging the development of modest solar installations throughout the state would also put less stress on the transmission and distribution grid, she said.

The shared approach has its roots in rural electric cooperatives, said Elaine Ulrich of the Department of Energy's SunShot program,

A Clean Energy Collective solar panel array in Denver. Such arrangements are drawing renters and apartment owners who prefer clean energy.

but has only begun to take off in recent years, and still accounts for a tiny fraction of solar production. There are at least 52 projects in at least 17 states, and at least 10 states are encouraging their development through policy and programs, according to the Solar Energy Industries Association, the main trade group.

It is among the profusion of financing mechanisms meant to encourage the development of solar energy, from residential leasing programs to crowdfunding.

The combination of plummeting prices for solar equipment and installation and generous federal and state incentives has widened their appeal. The Energy Department is encouraging their spread, publishing a guide to best practices in 2010, and is weighing proposals to award $15 million in grants to help design community projects.

In general, a developer builds a solar farm that can range from a few dozen panels on a rooftop to thousands sitting on more than 100 acres, and sells the electrical output of a set number of panels to each customer, depending on how much of their power use they want or can afford to offset. Customers then receive a credit for that power, often at a fixed rate per kilowatt-hour, that is then deducted from the energy portion of their electric bills.

Costs typically run $500 to $1,400 for a panel, said Paul Spencer, president of Clean Energy Collective, adding that customers benefit from the fact that the arrays can be situated in optimal locations to maximize energy production. But those costs can run higher in some markets, and customers must generally live within certain geographic or utility service boundaries.

The details vary from state to state, and can be complicated by how utilities charge customers. In Colorado, for instance, Xcel Energy customers continue to pay the standard nonenergy fees, but can buy enough solar shares to offset 120 percent of their load.

"I've been seeing a lot of zero bills," said Brendan Miller, a civil engineer who said he paid about $10,000 for 11 panels to cover most of his electricity needs in his Denver condominium.

Interested in solar energy since high school, Mr. Miller had purchased a system for his previous home in Arizona and said the community solar arrangement was much simpler because he did not have to navigate the tax credits or installation himself.

"It was more of a financial transaction than a contractor-construction transaction," he said.

In New York, the proposed system would allow customers to offset no more than 100 percent of their electric use and would limit their initial ownership period to five years for residential consumers and 10 years for businesses, with an option for renewal.

For customers, the systems offer flexibility, proponents say, because their interest in the panels is transferable so they can take the output with them if they move or turn it over to someone else. The community solar garden differs from another common way consumers can remotely buy green energy — energy service companies — because people like Mr. Miller buy into the array itself.

Still, they can carry high upfront costs depending on the size. For Mr. Polstein's roughly 3,000-square-foot house in Newton, for instance, it would cost about $41,000 — after anticipated rebates and incentives — to buy 32 panels in the coming Massachusetts array. He likes the idea of contributing to the growth of solar, but worries that he may end up, as an early adopter, paying more than he should.

"It may not be the smartest investment if you're only doing it from the point of view of money," he said. "But if you factor in the idea that you're trying to make a change in how the energy you use is produced and the effect it has on the world, then you can sort of rationalize it a little better even if five years from now you could do the same thing and it would cost a little less."

Why a Big Utility Is Embracing Wind and Solar

OPINION | BY JUSTIN GILLIS AND HAL HARVEY | FEB. 6, 2018

DENVER — Imagine planning your next trip and finding that Delta was selling first-class seats for less than the cramped middle seats in the back of the plane.

So you fly first class to New York and walk into the best French restaurant, only to discover that every dish is cheaper than the burger and fries down the street. Waiter, bring the duck à l'orange!

Fanciful as that might sound, something a bit like it is happening right now in the world of electricity.

Xcel Energy is a utility company with millions of electric customers in the middle of the country, from Texas to Michigan. In booming Colorado, the company asked for proposals to construct big power plants using wind turbines and solar panels.

The bids have come in so low that the company will be able to build and operate the new plants for less money than it would have to pay just to keep running its old, coal-burning power plants.

You read that right: In parts of the country, wind and solar plants built from scratch now offer the cheapest power available, even counting old coal, which was long seen as unbeatable.

Xcel, Colorado's biggest power company, has pitched a plan to regulators that will involve replacing two large coal-burning units with renewable energy and possibly some natural gas. The company expects to save tens of millions of dollars as a result. Power bills in Colorado have been falling recently, and they are likely to fall further with this plan.

So the plan will be cheaper, but why will it be better?

Because it will cut Xcel's emissions. That includes the carbon dioxide that is warming the planet, of course, but it also includes other pollutants, like the fine particles that can send children to the hospital with asthma attacks.

Turbines at the Spring Canyon Wind Farm outside Peetz, Colo. The farm is owned by Invenergy, and produces energy under contract to Xcel Energy.

Under the leadership of Benjamin Fowke, a gray-haired chief executive trained in finance, Xcel intends to get far ahead of the clean-power requirements that have been imposed by its regulators.

Across its eight-state system, Xcel predicts that well over half its electricity will come from renewable sources by the mid-2020s. It will be one of the cleanest large utility companies in the country.

Now, to be clear, the low bids that Xcel is getting include some federal subsidies for clean power. Those subsidies are entirely defensible, but both parties in Congress have agreed to phase them out in a couple of years. Mr. Fowke is jumping now in part to lock in the subsidized prices.

Yet costs for renewable technologies are coming down so much that by the time the federal subsidies expire, wind turbines and large-scale solar arrays will still be competitive in large parts of the country.

The same trend is occurring all over the world, even in countries that do not offer subsidies, with renewable projects routinely beating fossil-fuel projects in countries like Mexico and India. We are confident more price declines are coming.

The costs of huge batteries are also falling, and it looks as if they will turn out to be a big help in managing the variability of wind and solar power. Xcel is already testing a battery project near Denver, and it may buy more batteries as part of the new plan.

How, exactly, did the cleanest energy technologies get on a path to become the cheapest?

In a way, the story is as old as Henry Ford and his Model T, or in more recent times, the amazing progress of computer chips.

As they scale up, new technologies often follow a "learning curve" that cuts the cost. But it's not automatic. You have to build more and more units to drive the prices down.

That happened naturally with consumer products like Model Ts and cellphones, since everybody who saw the things wanted one. But the electricity system was a hidebound, monopolistic industry that used to spend virtually nothing on innovation.

For decades, utility executives who were wedded to coal regarded solar panels and wind turbines as expensive trinkets. But some far-sighted political leaders saw the potential as early as the 1970s.

President Jimmy Carter was one. Jerry Brown, then serving as California's youngest-ever governor, was another. Republican leaders in windy states, like Terry Branstad and Charles Grassley of Iowa, also got on board.

A combination of state clean-power mandates and federal subsidies helped to increase the market, as did similar policies in Europe. It has taken a couple of decades, but we are reaching a point where the new energy technologies are going to be cheap enough to drive a lot of the old coal-burning power plants off the market.

Nowadays, of course, the Trump administration is trying to take the country backward. It recently offered a scheme to subsidize coal and nuclear plants, but the plan was so ludicrous, a federal panel dominated by Trump appointees voted it down 5-0.

More ominously, the administration recently imposed costly tariffs on solar panels made in China. That is unquestionably bad for the solar industry, but we think it will turn out to be a temporary setback.

The real question now is how fast can the fossil-fuel plants be shut down. Even with favorable economics, human and institutional inertia is such that the remaining coal plants could take a long time to die.

States need to find ways to help utilities make the right decisions, perhaps by sharing some of the short-term costs of the shutdowns. They also need to protect workers who lose their jobs, and compensate communities that stand to lose part of their tax base.

Despite such concerns, the cost trends are clear, and inexorable. Mr. Fowke has positioned Xcel to take advantage of them, and a handful of other power companies across the country are taking similar steps.

But most utilities are still doing only what governments have required of them. With the best power plants becoming the cheapest, isn't it time for their leaders to seize the future, too?

JUSTIN GILLIS IS A CONTRIBUTING OPINION WRITER. **HAL HARVEY** IS THE CHIEF EXECUTIVE OF THE RESEARCH FIRM ENERGY INNOVATION.

Fuel From Landfill
Methane Goes on Sale

BY DIANE CARDWELL | OCT. 2, 2013

FARMERS, WASTE MANAGEMENT companies and the energy industries have long experimented with converting methane, a byproduct of decomposing organic matter, into transportation fuel.

Those efforts have met with mixed success, and a renewable natural gas fuel has not been widely available in the United States. But now, one leading supplier of natural gas transport fuel is taking a big step toward changing that.

Clean Energy Fuels will announce on Thursday that it has started selling a fuel made of methane from landfills and other waste sources at its more than 40 filling stations in California. The company, which is backed by T. Boone Pickens, is developing a nationwide network of natural gas pumps and plans to introduce the fuel elsewhere as well.

J. EMILIO FLORES FOR THE NEW YORK TIMES

Filling a Hertz bus tank with Redeem, a fuel made from rotting organic material, in Los Angeles.

The company expects to sell 15 million gallons of the fuel in California this year, more than double the amount of similar fuels the Environmental Protection Agency projected would be produced nationwide.

Its customers include companies like AT&T, Verizon, Mattel and Williams-Sonoma as well as large fleet operators like SuperShuttle and Hertz.

To many in the industry, the pace of the fuel's development has been something of a surprise.

"Though California and others have been investing in the development of this fuel, I don't think people were expecting there to be a significant public supply or access this soon — maybe not even this decade," said Tim Carmichael, who leads the California Natural Gas Vehicle Coalition, a trade group.

A big factor in methane's rise is the surge in natural gas production from shale drilling, which had already nudged the transportation industry to begin shifting to vehicles that can run on the cleaner-burning fuel, making it easier to meet emissions standards.

Another reason is powerful government incentives, especially in California, that have imposed strict regulations intended to help reduce carbon emissions to 1990 levels by 2020. Under the program, suppliers that reduce emissions during the production, transportation and use of the fuel are awarded tradable credits.

These and similar federal incentives are allowing Clean Energy to sell the fuel, which is called Redeem, at the same price as its conventional natural gas fuel even though it is more expensive to produce.

The new fuel is also cheaper than diesel fuel and it provides the companies some insulation from the geopolitics that can drive up petroleum prices.

But because of its source, the fuel counts as renewable and takes less energy to extract and process, making it more attractive to companies seeking to burnish their green credentials.

The fuel's environmental benefits also include capturing the methane before it is released into the atmosphere. When the methane-derived fuel is burned, it is far less harmful to the atmosphere than petroleum fuels. But the methane that escapes directly from decomposing waste is more potent as a heat-trapping gas than carbon.

For this reason, many large-scale farms, wastewater treatment companies and garbage companies have developed systems to capture escaping methane — known as biogas — for both transportation and electricity, and several start-up companies are working on systems of their own. There are projects in Europe as well, where biogas for transport is more common.

Although many of the methane-capture projects in the United States and Europe have been geared toward producing electricity, those markets have been declining, said Mackinnon Lawrence, principal research analyst at Navigant Research.

Looking to make transportation fuel was a logical alternative, he said, because producers can take advantage of federal and state incentives. The push has its risks, however, because the credit values have been so volatile that it is difficult for companies to commit to long-term investments.

Beyond the bottom line, customers are increasingly interested in how clean the fuel is, said Andrew J. Littlefair, the chief executive of Clean Energy, adding that Redeem can burn 90 percent cleaner than diesel. "We're seeing from these heavy-duty trucking fleets, and these shippers that hire these trucking fleets, they're really interested in sustainability," he said. "It's gotten to be a very important part of the sale."

John Simourian, chief executive of Lily Transportation, which uses a nationwide network of trucks to move a range of products, including construction materials and groceries, said that only a small portion of his fleet ran on natural gas but that the company was shifting over.

Not only is the fuel less expensive, but it gives the company a competitive advantage with customers on price and environmental concerns. "It's just a win all around," he said.

Harnessing the Net to Power a Green Revolution

BY BETH GARDINER | JUNE 18, 2013

LONDON — At the intersection of clean power and information technology, a new breed of digital start-ups is harnessing the power of the Internet to make smarter, more efficient use of energy and other resources.

Proponents call it "cleanweb," and they say the sector is poised to bring about huge leaps in efficiency, saving money and cutting planet-warming carbon emissions.

As its backers define it, cleanweb is any software or Internet application that makes it easier to use resources — like textiles or cars or electricity — more efficiently.

The label is applied to a diverse mix of companies, some of them far removed from the power sector. Cleanweb enthusiasts often point to Airbnb, a Web site that connects people seeking vacation accommodation with others looking to rent out their homes, reducing the use of hotel rooms — and, in theory, the number of hotels that need to be built.

The Nest, a sleek, smart home thermostat that can be controlled from a mobile phone, is cleanweb, too. So is Mosaic, a crowdfunding platform that links individual investors to solar energy projects that reduce the use of fossil fuels. RidePal tallies online votes from commuters to design routes to work for employer-funded buses, taking cars off the road in the congested San Francisco Bay area.

"For me, it's about bringing the optimism and the creative energy of the Web to the big challenges of sustainability," said Jack Townsend, an organizer of Cleanweb U.K., a network of British entrepreneurs and technology experts. "It's early days right now, but it's very fast-developing."

"A lot of the problems of sustainability are information problems, so information and information technology can be a big component of the solution," he said.

Investors scared off by volatility and falling prices in more traditional areas of clean technology — big wind farms or solar arrays that require hundreds of millions of dollars to get up and running — are turning in growing numbers to cleanweb, where capital requirements can be lower and returns can come quicker.

Globally, investors put at least $1.2 billion into cleanweb ventures in 2011, according to research by Pure Energy Partners and the Cleantech Group, a market research company. A quarter of clean technology deals had a cleanweb component that year, a 55 percent increase from 2009, said Nicholas Moore Eisenberger, the managing partner at Pure Energy Partners, a venture capital and strategy firm in New York.

Mitch Lowe, the managing partner at Greenstart, a San Francisco venture capital and design company focused on cleanweb, said the number of start-ups in the area had doubled in the past year.

"We're seeing a lot of interest in this category right now," he said. "The number of entrepreneurs who are starting businesses in this space has grown a lot in the last couple of years."

The growth of cleanweb is another example of the huge change information technology has brought to so many sectors of the economy, Mr. Lowe said. This time, he says, it is energy's turn to be revolutionized by the Internet.

"Cleantech is moving from its first chapter, where it was all about wind farms and solar panels and these huge industrial things," he said.

"Now that all that technology has been built, the question is how do you distribute it, how do you get it out to the world."

Fresh out of the University of Chicago's Booth School of Business, Archie Gupta, an electrical engineer, saw a way to help independent energy generators operate more efficiently. Big utilities have smart systems guiding their decisions about how much power to produce and when, but in the United States alone, there are 24,000 smaller-scale businesses and institutions — universities, hospitals, airports and factories — that also generate power, mainly for their own use, Mr. Gupta said.

Because energy is not their main business, many have not bothered to install sophisticated systems to manage it, he said. Root3 Technologies, a start-up that he co-founded a year ago, offers software and services to do just that.

"All the data is already there," he said. "We are taking the data and converting it into actionable information — and this is actionable information hour by hour. What do you need to do? What do you need to turn on? How much do you need to produce?"

"It's a significant bottom-line benefit," that helps clients cut their power generating costs by up to 30 percent, he said.

Along with leaders in the field like the entrepreneurs Sunil Paul and Blake Burris, Mr. Eisenberger, of Pure Energy Partners, recently helped to start the Global Cleanweb Initiative to promote the sector. In cities including Houston and Rome, the group has sponsored weekend meetings for programmers to brainstorm and build apps that save energy or other resources.

Information technology can have a bigger impact on resource management "than any hard technology in our lifetimes," Mr. Eisenberger said.

In addition to energy-related applications, the cleanweb world includes companies in what has been dubbed the "sharing economy," connecting individuals who want to share baby clothes, appliances, cars and more. That saves money as well as the cloth, metal and other materials used in manufacturing such goods — and the greenhouse gases their creation would have produced.

Brian Steel, the co-director of the Cleantech to Market program at the Haas School of Business, at the University of California, Berkeley, said the popularity of cleanweb could lead to a glut of companies in the area, followed by a shakeout and consolidation. Yet even if that happens, he said, the sector looks likely to play an important complementary role, alongside more traditional renewable power companies, in helping to cut carbon emissions and conserve resources.

Mr. Lowe, of Greenstart, said that venture capitalists who had lost money on clean energy investments in recent years might still be wary. But investors from outside the energy sector have been showing lots of interest, he said, looking at the new companies simply as strong start-ups with good prospects.

Greenstart is investing in one new cleanweb company every four weeks. "We're superbullish on it," he said: With a growing global population and tightening constraints on carbon emissions, "it's just a massive financial opportunity."

Mr. Eisenberger said he hoped the opportunities would draw even more entrepreneurs with big ideas.

"Instead of thinking about making a billion dollars by creating some sort of photo-sharing program, which is great," he said, "we would like that next generation of entrepreneurs to see how they can make a billion dollars using tech to tackle resource problems."

The Challenges of
Cleaning Up Cooking

BY BETH GARDINER | DEC. 8, 2015

MUSTAFABAD, INDIA — Khushboo Kushwaha has a few years before she will have to squat in front of a filthy, smoking open stove three times a day to cook meals for her family, as her older sister and cousins do now.

Khushboo is 11, and the girls in her home usually take up cooking duties as teenagers. But the smoke that billows from the wood and dried dung they burn, stinging the older girls' eyes and throats, already affects her.

The air in the semi-open courtyard of the Kushwaha family's home is heavy and choking. The older girls patiently prepare food for as long as six hours a day, sifting flour, rolling dough and tending to the vegetable and lentil dishes that bubble atop rough-hewn clay stoves.

"I don't like the smoke," Khushboo said. "I cough when food is being made," and her eyes get red.

About three billion people, more than 40 percent of the world's population, cook and heat their homes with dirty fuels like wood, dung and coal, burned on open fires or in traditional stoves, according to the World Health Organization. From China and Laos to Nigeria and Ethiopia, the resulting smoke prematurely kills about four million people a year, the organization says.

The smoky fuels, known as chula in India and biomass among scientists, are also a driver of climate change, in part because the black carbon particles they create absorb heat from the sun. It is not clear, however, whether a mass switchover to the alternative most readily available in India, liquefied petroleum gas, or L.P.G., would benefit the climate or be a small detriment, said Kirk Smith, professor of global environmental health at the University of California, Berkeley, and a leading voice on household air pollution.

From a health perspective, though, the pressing need for L.P.G. or other alternatives is clear, and renewable options like solar-powered cooking, while growing fast, are not yet widely available. It would be unconscionable for rich nations to demand "that the world's poor should bear the burden of lowering carbon emissions, when essentially minuscule increases would have such huge benefits," Dr. Smith said in an email. "It is not the cooking of the poor that threatens the climate, it is you and me."

India, the world's third-largest emitter of planet-warming greenhouse gases, is a key player at the climate summit meeting in Paris, and its leaders have long argued that they must prioritize improving the lives of the poor over tackling global warming. The competing agendas of wealthy nations, which have put most of the accumulated carbon dioxide in the atmosphere, and poorer ones worried that curbing their own growing emissions will hamper economic growth have long been a sticking point in efforts to reach a global climate deal.

About 700 million Indians, more than 55 percent of the country's population, rely on biomass stoves. Household air pollution is the second-biggest risk factor for death in India, and the third-biggest risk to health, causing stroke, heart disease, lung cancer, pneumonia and more, according to 2013 data from the landmark Global Burden of Disease study.

The suffering was apparent during a spring visit to Khushboo's mud-walled home, in a village near the northern city of Lucknow, where her family scrapes out a living farming wheat and potatoes. Her mother's vision is worsening, and she often feels too ill to cook, so an older daughter, Renu, 17, has taken up that responsibility.

Renu Kushwaha works beneath a bit of thatched roofing in a corner whose walls are black with soot. She suffers from dizziness and a constant headache.

Even the youngest knows what would solve their problems. "There's no smoke in a gas stove," Khushboo said. "It's much easier."

L.P.G., made up of propane and butane, is the cooking fuel families like the Kushwahas aspire to, smoke-free and far more convenient than the time-consuming chula. For many, though, L.P.G. is too expensive or simply unavailable, in part because India's poor infrastructure hampers distribution.

Improving that infrastructure is key. Also critical, Dr. Smith said, is an overhaul of India's L.P.G. subsidies, which largely go to the middle classes and the wealthy, not the rural poor who need them most.

Priti Kushwaha, a neighbor of Khushboo's family, has an L.P.G. stove, but says she uses it sparingly. Buying the fuel means a motorcycle trip of 10 kilometers, or 6.2 miles, and the process is so cumbersome she often has to go twice.

A canister of gas costs 665 rupees, or about $10, she says, a third of which is covered by a government subsidy. Priti Kushwaha, who is not related to the other Kushwahas, would love to cook with L.P.G. more often. "It is much easier to use the gas stove," she said. "It is just the inconvenience of getting it, and the cost."

She cooks most often with a wood- and dung-burning stove that is more modern, and much cleaner, than her neighbors' primitive ones. Provided by the Energy and Resources Institute, or TERI, a New Delhi-based research group, it is made of steel, with an electric fan that improves efficiency by forcing air into the burning chamber.

Increasingly, experts are seeing links between dirty fuels in the home and India's wider air pollution problem. About 25 percent of the country's outdoor pollution comes from households, said Kalpana Balakrishnan, a professor of environmental health engineering at Sri Ramachandra University in Chennai.

In the last 25 years, Venezuela, Chile and Costa Rica moved almost all households to L.P.G., Dr. Smith said. Ecuador did so in the 1990s and is now pushing for conversion to electric induction stoves, he said. Brazil achieved nearly universal gas use, but 10 percent of households returned to biomass when subsidies were scaled back, he said.

In India, more people are gaining access to L.P.G. But without a push from the government, it will take 20 to 30 years before gas and other clean-burning fuels are widely available, Dr. Balakrishnan said. "It's the vaccine analogy, it's the life-saving drug analogy," she said. "You don't wait for people to become rich before you get life-saving drugs to them. You step in and get them what they need."

From Oil to Solar: Saudi Arabia Plots a Shift to Renewables

BY STANLEY REED | FEB. 5, 2018

DHAHRAN, SAUDI ARABIA — Life in Saudi Arabia has long been defined by the oil that flows from the kingdom. Over decades, the vast wealth it pumped out paid not just for gleaming towers and shopping malls but also for a government sector that employs a majority of working Saudis.

Now, Saudi Arabia is trying to tie its future to another natural resource it has in abundance: sunlight.

The world's largest oil exporter is embarking, under Prince Mohammed bin Salman, on an ambitious effort to diversify its economy and reinvigorate growth, in part by plowing money into renewable energy. The Saudi government wants not just to reshape its energy mix at

CHRISTOPHE VISEUX FOR THE NEW YORK TIMES

Saudi Arabia's biggest solar farm in operation covers a parking lot of the national oil company, Saudi Aramco.

home but also to emerge as a global force in clean power.

Reaching that goal is a big if. But the strategy is finally making progress after fits and starts.

Riyadh on Monday tapped ACWA Power, a Saudi energy company, to build a solar farm that would generate enough electricity to power around 40,000 homes. The project will cost $300 million and create hundreds of jobs, according to Turki al-Shehri, head of the kingdom's renewable energy program.

By the end of the year, Saudi Arabia aims to invest up to $7 billion to develop seven new solar plants and a big wind farm. The country hopes that renewables, which now represent a negligible amount of the energy it uses, will be able to provide as much as 10 percent of its power generation by the end of 2023.

"All the big developers are watching Saudi," said Jenny Chase, an analyst at Bloomberg New Energy Finance, a market research firm.

"The country has made grand plans and pronouncements, but various bodies within it have failed to agree on the new way forward," Ms. Chase added. She referred to the agreement as "the first step in creating what is widely expected to be a major market."

Saudi Arabia has talked a big game when it comes to renewables. It adopted ambitious targets for green power several years ago, but no major projects were carried out, and little changed. That is not unusual.

The country's biggest solar farm in operation covers a parking lot of the national oil company, Saudi Aramco, here in Dhahran. Lying just a couple of miles from a fenced-off area honoring the country's first commercially viable oil well, it generates enough power for a nearby office block.

Still, the experiment with solar power has been an important catalyst, and the company built a team of experts in renewable power. The experience helped Saudi Arabia focus on conventional solar panels over another system, known as concentrated solar, in which mirrors focus sunlight to create heat.

The renewables strategy finally started to take real shape when Khaled al-Falih took over as energy minister in 2016. Mr. Falih made solar and wind a priority for the kingdom, and set up a new unit last year to expedite the work. Much of the staff was drawn from Aramco.

Mr. Shehri, who had worked at Aramco before leading the kingdom's renewables program, said he faced an "extremely challenging" task. Meeting Saudi Arabia's targets would require contracts for a series of new facilities to be awarded by the end of 2020. "The only way this was possible," he said, "was because we have done previous work."

Saudi Arabia, with its vast oil resources, would seem an unlikely champion for renewables. But the country's location and climate mean it has plenty of promising sites for solar and wind farms.

The costs of installing and operating those two technologies have fallen drastically around the world in recent years. That means that

What had been a scattering of small towns in Dhahran, Saudi Aramco's hometown, is now a major metropolitan area housing around four million people.

even in a country where oil is plentiful, renewables beckon as a cheap, and clean, alternative to traditional fossil fuels.

For the project announced on Monday, Riyadh received bids for the solar farm, which will be built in Sakaka, in northern Saudi Arabia, that rivaled the lowest ever submitted at auctions anywhere. At 2 to 3 cents per kilowatt-hour, a wholesale measure of electricity, solar power here would be below the cost of fossil fuel-generated electricity, Mr. Shehri said.

"Just look at the prices," Ms. Chase said. "That is why they are doing it."

A big push into wind and solar power would also have other benefits, notably allowing Saudi Arabia to sell more of its oil.

Saudis rely on air-conditioners for much of the year, and the scorching Arabian summer sends demand for power soaring. Much of that electricity today is generated at power plants fueled by oil. Last June, the facilities burned an average of 680,000 barrels of oil a day, according to data supplied by the Joint Organizations Data Initiative, a monitoring group.

That figure — comparable to the output of a modest-size oil-producing country like Egypt — was down from nearly 900,000 barrels a day in 2015, but it still essentially represents wasted cash. Had it been sold overseas, that crude could have added $47 million a day to government revenue, at current prices.

Selling oil internationally is central to funding the Saudi budget. The terms of the Sakaka project's auction required that developers pay the upfront cost of the solar farm, in return for payments for the power they supply to the grid. That would allow Saudi Arabia to continue focusing on producing and exporting oil while it makes the shift to cleaner power.

In the 1920s, the area surrounding the Aramco offices here was little more than a series of rocky hills. But then a team of American geologists discovered crude, and everything changed.

Dhahran is now home to the headquarters of one of the world's most advanced and prolific energy companies, with a series of research lab-

Dhahran is home to Aramco's headquarters, with a series of research laboratories, training centers and even a golf course on site.

oratories, training centers and even a golf course on site. What had been a scattering of small towns is now a major metropolitan area housing around four million people.

A major plank of the crown prince's plan to transform the Saudi economy involves finding jobs for young people. Attracting investment into what is essentially a nonexistent sector in the kingdom, Mr. Shehri said, would mean "creating jobs, creating manufacturing."

Still, despite the ambitious goals and positive language, the process by which Saudi Arabia has looked to expand its wind and solar capacity has raised concerns.

Analysts have pointed in particular to how Saudi leaders have chosen their preferred companies. When Riyadh produced a short list of two firms for the Sakaka project this month, it passed over one that had presented a lower bid than the finalists, leaving some experts worried about the transparency of the bidding process.

Local-supplier requirements might also deter some bidders. Mr. Shehri insisted that companies interested in the Sakaka project agree to spend 30 percent of the costs on domestic suppliers and expected that proportion to rise in subsequent bidding rounds. Many companies may find it difficult to justify building factories in Saudi Arabia just to construct one power plant.

The Saudi market's sheer size, however, means it merits the attention of the world's renewable energy companies. Paddy Padmanathan, the chief executive of ACWA Power, which also has other energy projects in the region, predicted in an interview last month that once the country's energy authorities became comfortable with renewables, they would ramp up their goals for wind and solar power production.

"Most of what they will procure going forward, I am convinced, will be renewables," he said.

Trading Pumps for Plugs: We Aren't There Yet

BY TOM ZELLER JR. | MARCH 30, 2011

KEVIN WALSH and his wife, Jeri Countryman, are young professionals in San Francisco with jobs requiring a fair amount of commuting. By himself, Mr. Walsh, a process engineer for a large international pharmaceutical company in San Carlos, Calif., logs a total of 43 miles each day.

With pump prices in the area creeping over $4 a gallon, the family was spending $200 or so a month on gasoline.

At the beginning of March, however, Mr. Walsh joined a tiny revolution, cutting the connection between his daily commute and foreign oil when he bought what is arguably the first plug-in electric car aimed at capturing the middle-American market: a Nissan Leaf.

"When available and practical, we make decisions to cut back on nonsustainable usage," Mr. Walsh, 38, said about his motives.

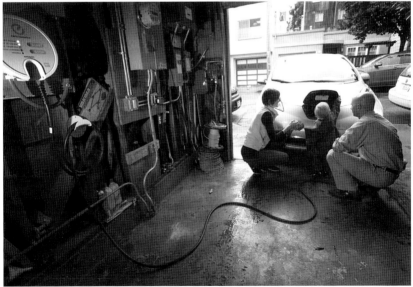

Kevin Walsh and his wife, Jeri Countryman, of San Francisco plugging their new Nissan Leaf electric vehicle into the charging station in their garage.

President Obama made it a campaign pledge, and later a goal of his administration, to put one million electric vehicles on the highways by 2015 and set aside more than $2 billion in the 2009 economic stimulus package for advanced battery and electric car research to help make it happen.

But the promise of an electric car revolution in the United States has come and gone before, and the question is where Mr. Walsh ends and mainstream America begins.

For electric car enthusiasts, the good news is that the right combination of technology and policy is now in place to ensure that plug-in cars are almost certainly here to stay — in some form. Battery range is longer, and government incentives are nudging consumers and industry to expand the market beyond the luxury niche it has occupied.

General Motors has just come out with the Chevrolet Volt, a gas-electric plug-in hybrid, and other consumer models, including the Ford Focus Electric and Toyota Prius plug-in, are coming.

"Things have really turned a corner," said Phyllis Cuttino, the director of the Pew Environment Group's Clean Energy Program. "There's just a whole broad segment of the population who now see how electric cars can work for them."

What's a little less clear, though, is just how quickly all this will unfold, and analysts seem to disagree over what it will take for electric cars to command any sizable portion of the market.

Part of the problem, said Robert Bryce, a senior fellow at the Manhattan Institute's Center for Energy Policy and the Environment, is that even at $4 a gallon, the price of oil still is not high enough to nudge mainstream Americans beyond the gasoline-fueled engines they know and love.

"The history of the electric car is the history of failure tailgating failure," Mr. Bryce said. "Maybe this time it will be different, but part of the problem isthat the energy density of gasoline is very nearly miraculous."

James Schlesinger, the former Energy Department secretary, put it more bluntly to the Web site Politico last month: "Anybody who's talking about energy independence is smoking pot," he said. "There's no way we're going to get to energy independence as long as we depend on the internal combustion engine."

Of course, early adopters with disposable income don't necessarily have to.

"I drove past the gas station the other day and gasoline was $4.19 a gallon," Mr. Walsh said. "My round-trip commute cost me less than a dollar in electricity that I produced on my own roof," he said, referring to the photovoltaic array he installed at his home four years ago.

That kind of enthusiasm is what's needed to lure the first wave, but electric cars like the Leaf still face hurdles to wider adoption, including a lack of public charging stations, the time it takes to charge (seven hours in most cases) and range limitations.

Faster-charging technologies are in the works, and a number of companies, including General Electric, Better Place and Coulomb Technologies, are vying to grab parts of the charging station market. As for range, the Leaf's battery permits a nominal driving distance of 100 miles on a full charge, though in actual traffic conditions that is likely to look something more like 60 or 70 miles.

For someone like Mr. Walsh, the Leaf works well. For other consumers, that might seem tenuous.

Sam Jaffe, an analyst with the market research firm IDC Energy Insights, said the other challenge for electric cars remains the upfront cost, which still exceeds comparably built conventional cars. A Leaf, for example, will be priced at about $33,600, Mr. Jaffe said, compared with Nissan's Versa model with roughly the same frame at about $15,000.

A federal tax credit for an electric car will shave $7,500 off the difference. But even if an electric car costs just pennies to operate, Mr. Jaffe said that's not enough for many buyers.

"What most people don't grasp is that in terms of operational costs — what it costs you to drive the car around — electric cars are advantageous today. You come out on top today. But people don't buy cars based on operating costs. They buy based on upfront costs."

Of course, it can take years before the lower operational cost makes up for the higher upfront cost of the Leaf. It would take Mr. Walsh, for example, almost five years to recoup the price difference between the Versa and Leaf.

So what's the market outlook?

In January 2010, the market research firm IHS Global Insight declared that "plugged-in vehicles" — a category that includes plug-in hybrids and fully electric vehicles — would make up 20 percent of the global market for light vehicles by the end of the decade. In November, Bloomberg New Energy Finance speculated that sales of such cars could hit 1.6 million, or 9 percent of the American market, by 2020 and perhaps 4 million, or 22 percent of the market, by 2030.

That would seem roughly in line with Mr. Obama's goal, but Mr. Jaffe thinks that's a bit unrealistic. He predicted that even by the end of 2011, only about 74,000 electric vehicles would be on the nation's highways, including conversions and street-legal golf carts. That would be out of a total of 250 million cars and trucks, or about 135 million traditional passenger cars, according to the latest government figures.

Mr. Jaffe estimates the number of electric vehicles will hit 885,000 by 2015. It's a solid, if modest number, and by then, most of the early adopters will have, well, adopted.

At that point, it will be up to everyone else. And at that pace of penetration, electric utilities should have enough time to work out systems for managing new demands on the grid. This will probably include lower off-peak prices, Mr. Jaffe said, to encourage electric car owners to charge their cars at night, when overall loads on the system are lighter.

For Mr. Walsh, such compromises ought to be taken in stride.

"While many people will argue about pollution and global warming, one way to look at it that I think many can agree on is that continuing to use fossil fuels and create air pollution is clearly not helping the environment," he said, "so why not make a better choice when it is available?"

The Challenge of Storing Energy on a Large Scale

BY ERICA GIES | SEPT. 29, 2010

SAN FRANCISCO — Renewable energy sources like solar power and wind have been in the spotlight lately, as have ways to improve control of the power distribution system through information technology. But another crucial component of developing a climate-friendly, secure and affordable supply of electricity — large-scale storage — has received little attention.

Now storage is stepping into the light. In the United States, incentives from the Energy Department, increased interest from venture capitalists and policy shifts at the state level, where utilities are regulated, are laying the groundwork for bringing energy storage capability to the electricity grid.

"Energy storage is the killer app for taking our grid to the next level," said Matt Rogers, a senior adviser to the U.S. energy secretary, Steven Chu.

Stored energy is part of daily life: batteries power cellphones and laptops, for example. But now the focus is on building grid-scale storage technologies. Possibilities include pumped hydroelectric energy; air compression systems; flywheels; and even superlarge batteries. These technologies can perform several desirable tasks in the energy system.

Grid operators must keep power flowing reliably to users, a task known as frequency regulation that has been complicated by the addition of unpredictable generating resources like solar and wind power. Those sources can change output rapidly if external conditions shift: a cloud crossing the sun or a drop in the wind.

Aside from these minute-to-minute changes in output, solar and wind also have larger production discrepancies: The sun does not shine at night, and in many places, wind is calm during the day. Energy experts call this "intermittency."

Utilities have generally used the more controllable output from fossil fuel power plants to compensate for intermittency. But if renewable sources are to contribute a greater share of the energy mix — California has a target of 33 percent by 2020 — the declining proportion of fossil fuel power available to smooth out the peaks and troughs of output will make storage technology essential.

"Well-meaning voters and legislators come up with things like 33 percent renewables in California by 2020," said Maurice Gunderson, senior partner at the venture capital firm CMEA Capital in San Francisco. "Well, it sounds like a good idea, but you really have to be a utility geek to get into the details and realize that it simply cannot be done without storage."

Mike Gravely, an energy research manager at the California Energy Commission, agreed. "There may be a point in the future where the policy requires renewables to bring storage along with them," he said.

Recent research suggests that storage technology could respond faster to supply and demand shifts than fossil fuel plants. Utility managers could address intermittency, Mr. Gravely explained, "with maybe half the amount of energy, if you have storage," than they would require using traditional generation.

Utilities must also build systems capable of meeting peak demand, which arises at different times of the day, week and year. For this purpose, utilities have traditionally relied on bringing additional fossil fuel generating plants into action.

But fossil fuel plants run most efficiently at full power. And the marginal plants turned on to meet peak demand are often less efficient and more polluting than the power generators that run around the clock.

Using stored energy to meet peak demand could eliminate the need to switch on dirtier, more expensive plants.

Depending on where storage is sited, it could also reduce the need for transmission lines, according to Jim Eyer, a senior analyst at the consulting company Distributed Utility Associates and a lead author of a report this year by Sandia National Laboratories on energy storage. That would be a boon because utilities often struggle to get rights of way to build transmission lines. As a result, they usually overbuild after they get permission.

"That's a waste of capital for something that might not be utilized for 20 to 30 years," said David MacMillan, president and co-founder of MegaWatt Storage Farms, an energy storage developer and adviser. "If you deploy storage, you don't have to add more transmission."

Storage can also help utilities get the best price for the energy they generate, using a strategy called "time shifting." Energy managers can store lower-cost energy produced at night, then release it to the grid during peak demand when it is more valuable. With both traditional power plants and wind farms, much more energy is produced at night than can be used.

"In West Texas, there is so much wind that, at night, they effectively have to let the things turn but dump the power because there's no demand for it," said Mr. Rogers of the U.S. Energy Department.

The Energy Department is supporting a variety of storage projects, using money from the economic stimulus funds approved by Congress.

"Today a storage solution costs about $1,000 per kilowatt- hour," Mr. Rogers said. "We're trying to drive it down to somewhere between $100 to $200 per kilowatt-hour."

The venture capital world has taken note. "Right now there's a big flock forming of grid-scale storage proposals, and that indicates that the entrepreneurs of America are responding to a very big opportunity," said Mr. Gunderson of CMEA Capital.

The most common technology already in use for grid storage is pumped storage hydroelectricity, in which managers use electricity to pump water up into higher elevation reservoirs at night, then release it at times of peak demand to recapture the energy. This technique proliferated in the United States during the heyday of nuclear plant construction in the 1960s and 1970s to absorb unused nighttime energy from reactors that produce a constant flow of power around the clock.

In 2009, the United States had 21.5 gigawatts of pumped storage generating capacity, according to the Energy Information Agency. Wider deployment, however, is limited by geography and environmental concerns similar to those associated with dams. The E.I.A. projects no change in capacity through 2030.

Another large storage option is compressed air. There is just one site operating in the United States at the moment, built in Alabama in 1991. But four new projects are in the works.

Electricity is used to force air under pressure into a cavern. To extract it, operators heat the compressed air with natural gas, then push it through turbines to generate electricity. Like pumped hydroelectricity, this method is limited by geography. And its use of natural gas produces emissions that undermine some of the benefits of turning to renewable sources.

A new flywheel project in New York will be used for frequency regulation because current models can store energy for only about 15 minutes. Flywheel systems use electricity to drive a motor, which accelerates a massive disc, storing electricity in the increased momentum. When the stored power is needed, the flywheel is used to drive the motor in reverse, generating electricity.

Batteries have not yet reached grid scale for the most part, although a village in Japan has assembled a bank of them to serve that purpose. Many experts think batteries hold the most promise because they are scalable and can be used anywhere.

"I've been deeply impressed by the new science in this space," Mr. Rogers said. With many battery technologies in development, he said he was confident that something economical would emerge.

New policies are also promoting energy storage in a drive to overcome barriers to its deployment. Those are needed because markets and regulators currently recognize just three types of businesses on the grid: generation, transmission and distribution.

"Storage is a peculiar animal; it's this funny, amorphous thing with some aspects of each entity," said Mr. MacMillan, the energy storage developer. "But market and regulatory structures have to adapt to take advantage of it."

That might happen soon. The Federal Energy Regulatory Commission is now considering ways in which it would set regulations for cost recovery for energy storage, perhaps by creating a separate asset class for storage.

A federal investment tax credit could also help compensate for the difficulties until the need for storage is more accepted, said Jason Makansi, executive director of the Coalition to Advance Renewable Energy through Bulk Storage, an advocacy group. Senator Ron Wyden, a Democrat from Oregon, sponsored such a provision in 2009 that, like most energy proposals, is currently languishing in Congress.

Some states have also introduced policies to promote storage.

The New York Independent System Operator has defined short-term energy storage devices like flywheels and batteries as frequency regulators, allowing them to participate in regulated markets. Independent system operators in Texas, California, and the Midwest, Mr. Makansi said, "have been progressively laying in policy, procedures, pricing, and other mechanisms that support deployment of storage services."

The California legislature recently passed an energy storage bill requiring the Public Utilities Commission to set storage targets. The bill is expected to be signed by Gov. Arnold Schwarzenegger by the end of September.

But advances are likely to be slow because of the inherent conservatism of the electric utility business.

"It's a business built on providing reliable service to customers," Mr. Makansi said.

"People will vote you out of office, as Gray Davis found, if you screw up the electricity system," he added, referring to the California governor who was ousted in 2003 after an energy deregulation scheme failed.

Coal's Continuing Decline

OPINION | BY JEFF NESBIT | FEB. 19, 2018

THREE SIGNAL FLARES went up for the American coal industry recently, all illuminating an inescapable conclusion: Despite President Trump's campaign promise, coal-fired power is in trouble and in all likelihood won't be reasserting itself in the United States. Nor should it.

The first signal, from the medical community, should give champions of "beautiful, clean coal" like Mr. Trump and his energy secretary, Rick Perry, pause. A research letter published in the Journal of the American Medical Association on Feb. 6 said that health professionals in Appalachian coal country were now finding the highest levels of black lung disease in coal miners ever reported.

The Coal Workers' Health Surveillance Program, administered by the National Institute for Occupational Safety and Health, or Niosh,

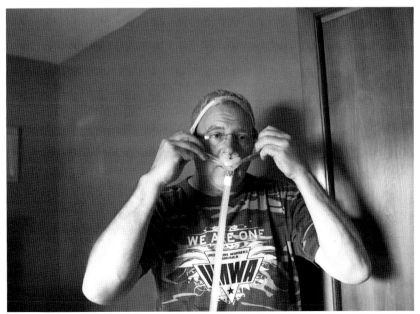

MADDIE MCGARVEY FOR THE NEW YORK TIMES

Dave Van Sickle, a retired miner, suffers from black lung disease and uses a breathing mask.

has offered regular chest radiographs for coal miners since 1970. By the late 1990s, black lung disease was "rarely identified" among miners participating in the program, researchers wrote. But a spike in cases in 2014, first reported by National Public Radio, prompted the federal agency to take a closer look at patients at three federally funded black lung clinics in southwest Virginia.

The agency was stunned by what it found. Black lung cases in Appalachia coal miners in those three clinics had skyrocketed. The disease was more severe. And coal miners were dying much younger than they had been two decades ago.

From January 2013 to February 2017, the Niosh researchers documented 416 coal miners among about 11,200 observed during the study with the most deadly form of the disease, progressive massive fibrosis, an advanced stage of black lung disease caused by inhalation of coal and silica dust at underground and surface coal mines. Miners with this advanced disease gradually lose the ability to breathe.

"We are seeing something that we haven't seen before," Ron Carson told NPR. He directs the black lung program for Stone Mountain Health Services, which treats coal miners from Kentucky, Virginia and West Virginia. The program went from seeing five to seven cases a year when it first opened in 1990 to 154 cases in the past year.

The reasons behind this sharp rise are complicated. But according to an NPR investigation, the most likely causes are the miners' working longer hours and their exposure to deadlier silica dust from cutting into rock to extract coal from thinner, harder-to-reach seams. The days of mining for readily available coal are long gone. It's more difficult, and seemingly more costly to miners' health, to extract coal in Appalachia now.

In 2014, a federal rule went into effect to improve protections for miners, including decreased allowable dust concentrations, but as the researchers noted, "Whether these added protections will decrease severe occupational lung disease in coal miners requires continued surveillance."

The second signal is subtle, but more damning. Despite the president's oft-repeated claim that coal-fired electricity generation is making a comeback, there is likely to be a significant number of retirements of coal plants this year, according to an assessment by the consulting firm S&P Global Marketplace Intelligence.

"Troubling economics have proven difficult to overcome, with low wholesale power and natural gas prices being the main contributing factors squeezing margins," S&P Global's assessment said. It added, "Coupling this unfavorable operating environment with an increasingly gas-, wind- and solar-focused resource mix going into the future will likely only continue to lower the need for an aging coal fleet."

Many of the coming coal retirements this year will happen in states President Trump won in 2016. A notable example is the Texas utility Vistra Energy, which said in October 2017 that it planned to retire three coal-fired power plants with a combined capacity of more than 4,000 megawatts. In Florida, the 1,252-megawatt St. Johns River plant shut down in early January, mainly because of market conditions. The utility plans to replace the coal plant's output with nuclear, natural gas and solar resources.

This development is in line with the findings of a report published last fall by the Union of Concerned Scientists, which concluded that "coal-fired power has become increasingly uneconomic and is the main factor driving the U.S. electricity sector to rapidly transition away from coal."

The third signal came from Mr. Trump's Energy Department. After the Federal Energy Regulatory Commission rejected a proposal from Mr. Perry, the energy secretary, last month to subsidize struggling coal and nuclear plants, he has apparently been exploring a new route to bail out coal companies like Murray Energy Corporation, whose owner, Bob Murray, is an important donor to the president.

Bloomberg reported recently that Mr. Perry was considering Energy Department payments to utilities like First Energy (which buys coal from Mr. Murray's company) to store coal reserves; that suggests that some coal companies might not survive without a federal bailout. A department spokesman said the report was not accurate, but when asked whether the agency could take its own action to keep coal and nuclear plants from retiring, the energy under secretary, Mark Menezes, told Bloomberg: "We have authorities that we can use when the need arises. They're well known. And we'll use them if we need to."

What seems clear from all three cases is that the coal industry isn't coming back. At best, Mr. Trump's administration can keep it on life support with taxpayer-funded bailouts. He should be embracing a clean, renewable energy future instead.

JEFF NESBIT IS THE EXECUTIVE DIRECTOR OF CLIMATE NEXUS, A NONPROFIT COMMUNICATIONS GROUP FOCUSED ON CLIMATE CHANGE AND CLEAN ENERGY, AND AUTHOR OF THE FORTHCOMING BOOK "THIS IS THE WAY THE WORLD ENDS."

What's Up in Coal Country: Alternative-Energy Jobs

BY DIANE CARDWELL | SEPT. 30, 2017

FROM THE MOUNTAIN hollows of Appalachia to the vast open plains of Wyoming, the coal industry long offered the promise of a six-figure income without a four-year college degree, transforming sleepy farm towns into thriving commercial centers.

But today, as King Coal is being dethroned — by cheap natural gas, declining demand for electricity, and even green energy — what's a former miner to do?

Nowhere has that question had more urgency than in Wyoming and West Virginia, two very different states whose economies lean heavily on fuel extraction. With energy prices falling or stagnant, both have

GEORGE ETHEREDGE FOR THE NEW YORK TIMES

Students playing soccer near a coal-fired power plant in West Virginia. As the state sheds coal jobs, local businesses and nonprofit groups are trying to create work in fields like alternative energy.

lost population and had middling economic growth in recent years. In national rankings of economic vitality, you can find them near the bottom of the pile.

Their fortunes have declined as coal has fallen from providing more than half of the nation's electricity in 2000 to about one-third last year. Thousands of workers have lost their jobs and moved on — leaving idled mines, abandoned homes and shuttered stores downtown.

Now, though, new businesses are emerging. They are as varied as the layers of rock that surround a coal seam, but in a twist, a considerable number involve renewable energy. And past jobs in fossil fuels are proving to make for good training.

In Wyoming, home to the nation's most productive coal region by far, the American subsidiary of a Chinese maker of wind turbines is putting together a training program for technicians in anticipation of a large power plant it expects to supply. And in West Virginia, a non-profit outfit called Solar Holler — "Mine the Sun," reads the tagline on its website — is working with another group, Coalfield Development, to train solar panel installers and seed an entire industry.

Taken together, along with programs aimed at teaching computer coding or beekeeping, they show ways to ease the transition from fossil fuels to a more diverse energy mix — as well as the challenges.

'ABSOLUTELY NO CATCH'

GILLETTE, WYO. — John Davila, 61, worked for 20 years at Arch Coal's Black Thunder Mine in Eastern Wyoming, a battered titan from an industry whose importance to the region is easy to see — whether in the sign in the visitors' center window proclaiming, "Wyoming Coal: Proud to Provide America's Energy," or in the brimming train cars that rumble out of the Eagle Butte mine on the outskirts of town.

But in April last year, at a regular crew meeting in the break room, he was among those whose envelope held a termination notice rather than a work assignment. "They called it a 'work force reduction,' " said

Mr. Davila, whose straight, dark ponytail hangs down his back. "Nice way to put it, but it still means you're out of a job."

So a summertime Thursday morning found him, along with a couple of dozen other men and women, in a nondescript lecture room at a community college, learning how a different source of energy, wind, might make them proud, too.

The seminar was the last of three that week organized by Goldwind Americas, which is ready to provide as many as 850 giant wind turbines for a power plant planned in the state. The company was looking for candidates, particularly unemployed coal miners like Mr. Davila, to become technicians to maintain and operate the turbines.

The program, which is to teach the basics of wind farm operation, maintenance and safety over two weeks in October, would cost the participants nothing but their time, organizers said. Those who wanted to test their potential would have a chance to climb a 250-foot tower that Saturday at a farm Goldwind owns in Montana. And if they completed

Watching a video at a Goldwind America seminar in Gillette, Wyo. The company recruits potential technicians to maintain and operate turbines at a power plant planned in the state.

the full program, they would have certifications that could open the door with any employer they chose.

"There's absolutely no catch — you don't like me, you don't like Goldwind, that's O.K.," David Halligan, the company's chief executive, told an even larger crowd in Casper the day before. "There's going to be opportunity across the country."

It is a message of hope that has been in short supply, especially after the loss of more than 1,000 jobs in the region and the bankruptcies last year of three major producers. But while coal's prospects have been dying down, wind development is poised to explode in the state, which has some of the world's strongest and most consistent winds. And while coal mining jobs have fallen to historic lows nationally in recent years, the Bureau of Labor Statistics predicts that wind-energy technician will be the fastest-growing occupation, more than doubling over the next seven years.

Though most of the coal jobs lost last year have since returned as companies have emerged from bankruptcy, the insecurity surrounding the industry remains. "It's been a little scary when you've got people all around you getting laid off," Brandon Sims, 37, an Air Force veteran who works for an explosives company that serves the mines, said outside the lecture room. "You never really know when your day to get the pink slip is."

HANDS-ON PRACTICE

HUNTINGTON, W.VA. — Coal mining was already dead in Crum, a town of less than 200 just this side of the Kentucky border, by the time Ethan Spaulding, 26, graduated from high school, he said. That dashed his hopes of becoming a roof bolter, helping stabilize the ceilings of mine tunnels. "You don't even have to have a high school diploma to go to the coal industry," he said, "and you can start making $150,000 a year." Or perhaps you once could.

Mr. Spaulding was standing near the railroad tracks at the edge of town where trains move coal out of the region, behind a dilapidated

Corey Adkins, 32, in the greenhouse at Coalfield Development's West Edge Factory in Huntington, W.Va. The greenhouse is part of an agriculture program that is to include a solar-powered fish farm.

brick building that once housed a high-end suit factory. It is becoming a hub for the family of social enterprises that Coalfield Development leads, which include rehabilitating buildings, installing solar panels, and an agriculture program that grows produce and is turning an old mine site into a solar-powered fish farm.

Wanting to stay in Crum, Mr. Spaulding went through the solar program Coalfield runs with Solar Holler, which offers its participants a two-and-a-half-year apprenticeship. He is now a crew chief at the training center, overseeing the renovation of a larger classroom inside the building. Though he is optimistic that he can eventually reach his target income in the solar industry, the installation jobs for which the trainees will ultimately qualify generally pay far less — $26 an hour, on average, nationally.

And yet there is keen interest. For David Ward, 40, managing installations at Solar Holler helps repay the student loans he ran up pursuing a degree in counseling — a growth industry in a state reeling from opioid addiction. An electrician, he said he was "interested in the idea of making your own power and the environmental impact."

The program is the brainchild of Brandon Dennison and Dan Conant, two West Virginians who wanted to help develop a sustainable economy in the state. Mr. Dennison, 31, started Coalfield Development in 2010; it grew out of a volunteer effort to build low-income green housing. Mr. Conant, 32, had worked on political campaigns, including Barack Obama's first presidential contest. After becoming involved in the solar industry, he concluded that rooftop solar development, with its individual, decentralized nature, could combine the door-to-door approach of political campaigning with a technology to fight climate change.

He completed the first Solar Holler project — putting panels on the Presbyterian church in his hometown, Shepherdstown, on the Potomac River — and, quickly overwhelmed with demand for similar installations, realized the state didn't have a work force to handle it. So he formed a partnership with Mr. Dennison's organization to develop one. At Coalfield's facility here, participants learn how the arrays create electricity and connect to the power system, but they also get practice installing panels on a shed behind the main building. That helps them clear one of the basic industry hurdles: becoming comfortable working on a roof.

A VIEW MOST NEVER SEE

SHAWMUT, MONT. — If a big worry for would-be solar installers is staying balanced while ferrying heavy glass-sheathed panels around a roof, for potential wind energy technicians it is whether they can climb more than 200 feet in broiling heat or icy cold and emerge into the gusts to fix machinery. Still, the Goldwind technicians say working so high up is one of the job's best features.

"You get a view that most people will never see," as Lukas Nelson, 27, a site manager in Ohio, put it in one of the company's promotional videos. Only a few towers have elevators, and at Goldwind's power plant here, the access is by a series of 90-degree aluminum ladders and steel mesh platforms, straight to the top.

It was Saturday morning after the three seminars, and Goldwind safety managers had delivered a brief lecture in a trailer that served as the farm office, warning of perils like rattlesnakes in the tall grasses outside and electrocution from throwing switches in the towers.

The organizers separated the crowd of about 20 into two groups. One would take a tour of the wind farm and substation while the other climbed towers whose blades sat idle. After lunch, they would switch.

In front of the trailer, Chancey Coffelt, 33, Goldwind's regional safety manager, was showing the climbing group how to put on harnesses — a network of heavy metal clips and rings attached to straps that thread over the shoulders, across the chest and around each thigh. They would latch onto a rope pulley system as they climbed each of four ladders and then hook into a bracket as they reached each

Members of a training group putting on harnesses before climbing a wind tower in Shawmut, Mont.

platform before freeing themselves from the pulley.

Mr. Davila, the 20-year mine veteran, was standing with members of the second group, chatting about Wyoming's wobbly energy economy and how wind might — and might not — steady it. "A lot of coal miners don't like wind or solar, but you need them all," Mr. Davila said. "It's like a puzzle you have to solve: just think about how many things we plug in."

Still, many of the men expressed concern over what the jobs would pay, saying the salaries paled in comparison to what they could earn on an oil rig, for instance.

"It's so easy to get a six-figure job in the oil industry," Jesse Morgan, a baby-faced 31-year-old city councilman and back-office worker at a drilling services company, had said over beers at a bar in Casper where he was asked to show ID. "You get addicted to that money."

But it could be worth taking a pay cut to get out from under the stress of constantly planning for the next layoff, and being able to return home at night rather than working 30- to 40-day stints offshore. The oil field never stops, Mr. Morgan said of his time on the rigs. "It's 24/7 — you miss birthdays, every holiday."

As with the other men, Mr. Morgan's work experience made him an attractive candidate for Goldwind. Accustomed to the industrial behemoths of fossil fuel production, he is familiar with the environment, equipment and procedures of working safely while surrounded by danger — like remembering to fasten the chin strap on a hard hat so it won't slip off and injure a colleague laboring hundreds of feet below.

Chelsae Clemons, 26, a technician at a Goldwind plant in Findlay, Ohio, said the emphasis on safety and training was part of the program's value. Among the few staff members at the seminars with a bachelor's degree, she had worked in a lab at a hospital and had little relevant experience when she decided to pursue a career in renewable energy. In Gillette, she told the crowd, "They're giving certifications I had to pay for."

HINTON, W.VA. — "Solar's not going to be everything, and one of the big challenges for the state is how do we diversify and get lots of cool stuff going," Mr. Conant, the Solar Holler founder, was saying as he drove from a solar installation at a hilltop farmhouse toward a 1940s summer camp that the local coal company provided for the children of its employees until 1984. "When you've been a one-industry town for a really long time, that's an issue. The last thing we would want to do is pin our hopes on doing that again, just with some other technology."

After winding down a road canopied by emerald-green trees, he passed the opening of the Great Bend Tunnel, during whose construction in the 1870s, as one legend tells it, the African-American folk hero John Henry beat a steam drill in opening a hole in the rock, only to die from his efforts. Minutes later, Mr. Conant came to Camp Lightfoot, which a nonprofit organization, Appalachian Headwaters, is turning into an apiary with an eye toward helping displaced coal workers and

GEORGE ETHEREDGE FOR THE NEW YORK TIMES

Sean Phelps in beekeeping gear at Camp Lightfoot in Hinton, W.Va. A nonprofit group is converting the former summer camp to honey production to help displaced coal workers.

military veterans get into the honey business. Early next year, Mr. Conant plans to install solar panels on an old gymnasium, which now holds racks of wood frames for the hives.

Deborah Delaney, an assistant professor of entomology and wildlife ecology who oversees the apiary and bee program at the University of Delaware, said the area was well suited for a honey enterprise. It is largely forest, unsullied by the pesticides that threaten the insects in industrial farm areas, and it has plant species like black locust and sourwood whose honey can fetch a high price.

"This is bee paradise," she said, sitting on the porch of the cafeteria building where a Patriot Coal banner hung askew on one wall. For now, Ms. Delaney and the program's staff are getting the colony established on a hillside in 86 hives that buzz away behind electrified wire fencing to protect them from bears. Next spring, they plan to distribute about 150 hives to 35 beekeepers either free or through a low- or no-interest loan. Come harvest time, the beekeepers would bring their honey-laden frames to the camp for extraction and processing; organizers would pay them for their yield and then sell the honey to support the program.

"For some people it might be a side hustle, but for other people it could really turn into, over time, a true income that could sustain a family," said Kate Asquith, program director at Appalachian Headwaters.

Economists say this kind of diversification is important, especially in a region where coal is unlikely to make a major comeback, even if Trump administration policies are able to foster a revival elsewhere. Demand is strongest for the low-sulfur coal from the Powder River Basin straddling Wyoming and Montana, rather than what Appalachia produces. The new-energy industries cannot replicate what coal once did, economists say. Long-term jobs at the Wyoming wind farm would number in the hundreds at best, while the solar program thus far trains only 10 workers each year.

Even a coal boom wouldn't create jobs the way it used to: Like the steam drill that ultimately took John Henry's place, new equipment and technologies have replaced workers in heavy industries. Production of coal, for instance, increased over all from the 1920s until 2010, while the number of jobs dropped to 110,000 from 870,000.

So interest in the bees has been high here. "Thought it was weird at first — bugs in a box in the backyard," said Sean Phelps, 27, who left a secure job as a school janitor to work with the bee program. Exposure to his father-in-law's hives changed his perspective. Now he sees them as a way to help the area, as well as fun. "This is what I want to do," he said. "Whenever you're out in them, it reduces a lot of stress."

INTERRUPTED BY A STORM

SHAWMUT, MONT. — It was after lunch, and Mr. Davila and Mr. Morgan were at the base of one of the wind towers, wearing heavy harnesses and waiting for the first group to finish so they could start the climb. Suddenly, Jason Willbanks, 39, who lost a job as an electrician with a coal company and now drives crews to and from their shifts on coal trains, emerged from within. Walking heavily into the blazing sunlight, he clattered onto the metal platform and stairs. Asked how he was, he shot back: "Sweating like a fat guy at an all-day dance."

As he pulled off the harness, dropped to his knees in a patch of shade on the grass and rolled onto his back, Mr. Davila offered him a bottle of water from a cooler. "You've earned it," he said.

Not long after, word came from the Goldwind crew: A thunderstorm was heading toward the farm, so the second group could not climb.

"I feel like I'm all dressed up with nowhere to go," Mr. Davila said, disappointed, gesturing toward the harness. "I wanted to see if I could get up."

"You've just witnessed what it's like to be a wind-turbine technician," Mr. Coffelt, the safety manager, said, cocking an ear over one shoulder and suggesting that the group move away from the rattlesnake he had heard. "Imagine if you're one or two stacks up when you get that alert: right back down we come." After weighing options, the Goldwind organizers called it a day, offering repeated apologies and promises to get the men back to the site which, over the following months, they did.

Mr. Morgan, who posted a beaming selfie from atop the turbine on Facebook, did not apply for the training program. But Mr. Davila did, and was accepted.

He is torn over whether to enroll, he said. He is desperate for the work but hesitant to leave his wife and home in Gillette, where he has lived since he was 6, for one of the jobs immediately available outside the state. Still, he added with a chuckle, it might be good to move: "Maybe there's more to the world than Gillette."

CHAPTER 4

Clean Energy Controversies

Clean energy is vital to an increasingly warm and crowded world. But even clean energy has its difficulties. Whether it's marketing issues, environmental issues, unforeseen effects on health, employment or local versus big business, clean energy brings with it negative consequences as well as positive ones. Until newer clean energy methods become more effective and widespread, the way it is produced and distributed will continue to be controversial.

Fight to Keep Alternative Energy Local Stymies an Industry

BY DIANE CARDWELL | MARCH 23, 2016

COWGILL, MO. — Up and down the center of the country, winds rip across plains, ridges and plateaus, a belt of unharnessed energy capable of powering millions of customers, with enormous potential to help meet national goals to stem climate change.

And because the bulk of the demand is hundreds of miles away, companies are working to build a robust network of high-voltage transmission lines to get the power to the coasts.

If only it were that simple. In all, more than 3,100 miles of projects have yet to be built, in need of government approval.

One of the most ambitious projects, called the Grain Belt Express from a company called Clean Line Energy Partners, spent six years

Jeff Gatrel at his farm in northern Missouri. The Gatrels are part of a group of local land-owners who oppose a plan to build high-voltage transmission lines across or near their property to get power produced from wind to the East Coast.

winning the go-ahead in three of the Midwestern states it would cross, only to hit a dead end in Missouri when state regulators voted 3 to 2 to stop the project. They were swayed by landowners like Jennifer Gatrel, who runs a midsize family cattle operation with her husband, Jeff, here in the northwestern part of the state.

She and other opponents made the usual arguments against tram-pling property rights through the use of eminent domain, obliterating their pastoral views and disrupting their way of life.

But they also argued something else: Why should they have to live beneath the high-voltage lines when there is plenty of wind in the East?

Now the whole project is waiting, putting the Gatrels in the middle of an emerging battle over how the nation should shift to renewable energy and meet ambitious targets in carbon reduction. The outcome will determine where and how green energy will develop over the coming decades.

"We have this potential for high-quality renewables in real volume for the first time," said James J. Hoecker, a former chairman of the Federal Energy Regulatory Commission who now advises the transmission industry. "The problem is, where the best renewables are, there are few customers."

The transmission lines like Grain Belt Express, he said, would bring the electricity to where there is demand.

The push to enhance the grid has gained urgency as renewables have spread. Already, electric systems in areas like Hawaii and Germany are under strain as wind and solar power fluctuate and overload the wires. What is needed, proponents say, is a new infrastructure better suited to handle renewable energy.

Energy Department officials acknowledge as much, saying that the United States must significantly upgrade its transmission and distribution system to meet both the needs of the information economy and clean energy goals, an effort that would require an estimated $900 billion in investment by 2030.

A recent study by the National Oceanic and Atmospheric Administration and the University of Colorado, Boulder, found that with such a network, the United States could supply most of its electricity with renewables by then at costs near today's prices and get close to meeting the goals set in the Paris agreement on climate change.

But opponents like Ms. Gatrel say that giant projects like the Grain Belt Express represent an outmoded, centralized approach to delivering energy. Just as it is healthier and more sustainable to eat foods close to where they are grown, the argument goes, so, too, should electricity be consumed closer to where it is produced.

"We believe that the East Coast has access to abundant offshore wind and that any time you talk about green or clean, you should also be talking about local," she said. "Unnecessary long-haul transmission lines are not our country's future."

It isn't just here in northwestern Missouri that construction of new power lines has met resistance, and transmission projects can live or die at the hands of state and county officials representing the local interest.

Clean Line has five projects in the works, including one that failed to gain approval in Iowa and another that ran aground in Arkansas and is awaiting federal approval under a thus-far unused provision of the 2005 Energy Policy Act. TransWest Express, a connector that the billionaire Philip Anschutz is proposing to install from the enormous wind farm he is developing on his south-central Wyoming cattle ranch to Las Vegas, is also awaiting a federal go-ahead.

But some energy officials and executives say there is a more dynamic and resilient alternative to these sprawling networks. Instead, they are promoting the development of less centralized systems that link smaller power installations, including rooftop solar, storage and electric vehicles, an approach known as distributed generation.

Conflict over those competing visions has cropped up across the country in fights over both wind and solar developments, but nowhere is that conflict starker than in Missouri's rejection of Grain Belt.

The transmission line, which could create thousands of temporary manufacturing and construction jobs in the state, attracted strong support among some economic development officials and landowners. They saw it as a chance to bring needed revenue to local counties and school districts, as well as to provide extra income for those whose land it crosses.

"I'm wanting to make sure that my local district has the assets to be able to do what they need to do," said Wayne Wilcox, 68, who runs a farm that has been in his family since 1884 and is a commissioner in Randolph County. "I just believe a project like this brings a lot of good to a community."

But opponents flooded the state Public Service Commission with thousands of comments against the proposal. Among the objections was granting Clean Line eminent domain so it could profit from shipping electricity to energy-hungry regions that command higher power prices. In addition, opponents say that the lines can interrupt farming operations, pierce the country quiet with humming or popping sounds and pollute the nights with a glow.

Forging at Hubbell, a supplier of power system equipment in Centralia, Mo. Proponents of a transmission line to take wind power east say it could create temporary manufacturing and construction jobs in the state at places like Hubbell.

And although the lines are said to be safe, farmers are warned not to refuel vehicles underneath them, or if refueling is necessary, to ground equipment with heavy chains.

Michael Skelly, Clean Line's president and founder, said that the lines would not glow, but acknowledged that most landowners wouldn't be eager to have the towers, which could rise 150 feet, on their properties. He also said that the exceptional winds of the Great Plains could go a long way toward reducing the country's carbon emissions, and that the company would compensate landowners for mission-building program, he said, it was up to private companies to devise business models to handle it.

"The difficult thing is that with infrastructure of any type, it has to go somewhere," he said, adding, "To motivate investors, there has to be a possibility that they make money — otherwise, it's not going to happen."

The state's five-member Public Service Commission, which rejected the proposal by one vote, concluded that its priority was Missouri, and "that any actual benefits to the general public from the project are outweighed by the burdens on affected landowners."

One of the dissenting commissioners, Daniel Y. Hall, who is now the chairman, wrote that the majority had used an "overly narrow and parochial interpretation of the public interest" that put the state "on the wrong side of history."

That debate is far from over. Clean Line plans to reapply, Mr. Skelly said, and Ms. Gatrel and her neighbors have vowed to continue their fight.

Last month, she stood on a windswept hill at her home, just below a flock of chickens and ducks pecking near a cold frame holding the last of a crop of lettuce. Her son, Dalton, ran a pony around a ring while her husband, who like his wife is 35 years old, worked cattle on horseback in a nearby pasture.

"I love this life," she said. "I love this land."

Solar Trade Case, With Trump as Arbiter, Could Upend Market

BY DIANE CARDWELL | JUNE 30, 2017

MILLIONS OF AMERICANS now get their electricity, at least in part, from the solar panels that have rapidly spread throughout the country since 2010, thanks to their sharply declining cost. For customers — including homeowners, businesses and utilities — as well as for the companies that promote and install them, cheap solar panels have been a good thing.

But for American manufacturers, those cheap panels — specifically, a glut of low-cost supplies from overseas — have not been a good thing, driving more than a dozen of them to the brink of bankruptcy and beyond.

Now, manufacturers are fighting back, in an unusual trade case that could put the final decision about government intervention, and any remedy, directly in President Trump's hands.

The case, filed with the United States International Trade Commission, is shaping up to be one of the first major trade decisions of the Trump administration. The outcome could have a powerful impact on whether the American solar industry will be able to compete on cost with conventional fuels like natural gas and coal in producing electricity.

And China, Mr. Trump's frequent foil on trade issues, has interests on both sides of the fight.

The cheaper equipment coming into the American market is often from Chinese manufacturers that the trade commission previously determined were dumping goods below cost, according to the petition. But the company that initiated the new case, Suniva, is an equipment maker based in Georgia whose majority owner is a Chinese company.

The petition seeks steep tariffs and minimum price guarantees on certain solar energy equipment made outside the United States. The commission is set to vote on the merits of the case by Sept. 22, and send any recommendations to the president by Nov. 13. But it is already reshaping the market.

Prices for solar panels have increased as buyers rush to get ahead of potential tariffs. Solar-farm developers have become skittish about long-term commitments to supply power at prices that could become uneconomical if tariffs, which can be applied retroactively, raise their costs.

"It clearly throws a wrench into what is already a challenged global market," said Shawn Kravetz, president of Esplanade Capital, a hedge fund based in Boston that is focused on solar energy companies. "There are going to be winners and losers. The list of losers is long."

Though Suniva, once lauded on the White House blog as "an American success story" during the Obama administration, originally filed the petition in April, it is in many ways the next skirmish in a protracted war between the United States and China that started in 2011. The dispute centers on crystalline silicon cells, the major electricity-producing components, as well as the modules, or panels, into which they are assembled.

Back then, SolarWorld Americas, a subsidiary of a now-bankrupt German panel maker, filed a trade complaint along with six other domestic solar manufacturers that accused their Chinese counterparts of using unfair government subsidies to finance their operations and then selling their merchandise for less than the cost of manufacturing and shipping it.

SolarWorld, which has joined Suniva's petition, won that battle, as well as a second case that included Taiwan, where Chinese manufacturers had turned for cells to avoid anticipated tariffs.

After the imposition of tariffs beginning in 2012 that ranged from about 20 percent to about 55 percent for the largest cell and panel makers, manufacturers outside China and Taiwan — including those in the United States like SolarWorld and Suniva — saw their fortunes rise. In 2014, SolarWorld Americas, based in Oregon, announced a $10 million expansion of its plant and plans to hire hundreds more workers to meet surging demand for solar panels.

Suniva had grown out of government-supported research at Georgia Tech to become one of the largest American makers of solar cells and finished modules. But the much larger Chinese manufacturers that came to dominate the global market kept up the pressure on price. Seeking a much-needed infusion of cash to finance an anticipated expansion, Suniva sold a majority stake in 2015 to a Chinese company, Shunfeng International Clean Energy, which wanted to get a foothold in what it believed was a growing American market.

Then came a glut of cheap, new panels as Chinese manufacturers began operating or contracting with factories in countries like Malaysia, Thailand and Vietnam, the petition charges. Last year, the Chinese government suggested it might slash its domestic incentives for buyers of solar panels, sharply reducing demand for equipment and adding to the oversupply. Manufacturers cut their prices to compensate, which sent global prices plummeting. Even though China ended up shaving subsidies just slightly and only for large power-plant arrays, prices remained low.

As panel prices dropped to about 40 cents per watt in late 2016 from 57 cents per watt in 2015, American solar installations reached a record high, making solar energy the biggest source of new electricity generation last year. But the domestic industry's share of the panel market, which had been declining since 2013, tumbled to 11 percent in 2016 from 17.1 percent the previous year, according to the market research firm IBISWorld.

In those conditions, Suniva could not compete as a supplier. Starting in March it shuttered its two factories in Michigan and Georgia, laying off about 250 workers, and in April it filed for Chapter 11 bankruptcy protection. About a week later, it secured a loan from one of its creditors to pursue the trade case.

With control of Suniva in the hands of the bankruptcy court, Shunfeng declared in May that it no longer supported the company's trade case, saying it was "not in the best interests of the global solar industry." It said in March that it would take a charge of roughly $38 million on its Suniva investment, though it could still benefit if the company prevails in the case.

Suniva argues that because of the global nature of the solar trade, the American manufacturing industry needs blanket safeguards from the trade commission that would apply to the crystalline silicon cells and modules manufactured anywhere outside the United States. It is the only way, the complaint argues, to keep manufacturers from circumventing tariffs aimed at specific countries by setting up shop elsewhere.

Without global relief, the domestic industry will be playing Whac-a-Mole," the petition says. "The way that the world's largest producers have reacted to antidumping and countervailing duty claims demonstrates that global relief is required."

But opponents say the case threatens many of the hundreds of thousands of workers whose jobs could be eliminated in an industry slowdown. Those include people who install, finance and oversee the development of large-scale solar projects, as well as manufacturers of support structures for the panels and devices that regulate the flow of electricity from them.

According to a report from GTM Research, a consultant firm that tracks the solar industry and provides data and analysis for the industry's main trade group, the Solar Energy Industries Association, which is aggressively fighting the petition, a finding in Suniva's favor could reduce expected installations over the next five years by 50 percent.

Adding to anxiety in the industry is the potential role of Mr. Trump, who would have broad leeway to determine how to proceed should the commission find that the domestic industry had been harmed by the surge in imports.

Though the president has pledged to increase manufacturing jobs, he has not offered the same full-throated support as his predecessor for solar energy. Proponents see solar energy as an important weapon in the fight against climate change, making its ability to compete economically with conventional sources — a concept known as grid parity — even more critical.

"Grid parity is of the utmost importance, so that we are competing on price and price alone," Abigail Ross Hopper, chief executive of the solar trade group, said. "If you change the underpinnings of that, it undermines what we're doing."

If things go Suniva's way, analysts say, other domestic manufacturers could also benefit, although the industry would most likely contract over the next few years.

Two makers of crystalline silicon cells and panels, SunPower and Solaria, are expanding their production capacity at factories in California. Then there is First Solar, based in Tempe, Ariz., which is also expanding production at its factory in Perrysburg, Ohio. The company mainly manufactures in Malaysia, but it uses a different technology and would not be subject to the trade restrictions. And if Tesla is able to get its troubled and much-delayed panel factory in Buffalo up and running, it could benefit as well.

Then, too, the major Chinese manufacturers are already exploring options for opening their own factories in the United States, said Ocean Yuan, chief executive of Grape Solar, a distributor of panels based in Eugene, Ore.

"There's no other way for them to enter the U.S. except that they make panels in the United States," he said. "So, I guess that's the positive side."

Reconciling Clean Energy and Conservation

BY JOHN LORINC | OCTOBER 1, 2009

WITH RENEWABLE ENERGY poised for explosive growth, some conservation groups are racing to advance policy proposals and guidelines meant to prevent wind and bioenergy producers from despoiling sensitive habitats, especially in the prairie grasslands of the Midwest.

The Nature Conservancy, which this year sounded a warning about "energy sprawl," is working with state energy officials and wind firms to build a database of maps that indicate wetlands and habitats within gusty regions. "We can tell the industry, these are places to avoid," said the organization's head of energy, Jimmie Powell.

A recent article in the conservancy's magazine says that conservation scientists have come to understand that turbines fragment the habitats of ground nesting birds like sage grouse and prairie chicken. "It's avoidance behavior," Mr. Powell said, because the towers are perceived as roosts for raptors.

Last fall, the wind industry and leading naturalist groups established the American Wind and Wildlife Institute, to do research, develop mitigation strategies and create incentives for companies that comply. Next month, the federal Fish and Wildlife Service is expected to release siting guidelines for wind farms on federally owned lands, but Mr. Powell says private land is a much more significant issue.

Among the Nature Conservancy's recommendations for wind developers:

- Avoid locations that require new transmission corridors.
- Take landscape integrity into account.
- Require location scouts working for wind farm developers to consult with regional wildlife authorities before consummating lease arrangements.

- Direct wind farm development onto established agricultural lands.

Mr. Powell added that the latest research suggests bats are drawn into the vortex created by turbine blades, which causes their lungs to explode. The conservancy is also developing operator guidelines that could involve measures like pausing blade rotation in periods when the wind isn't blowing at economically viable speeds.

On the biofuel front, a team of scientists representing various national conservation groups and the University of Minnesota released a study proposing a framework for assessing the environmental impacts of current and future bioenergy production, also on a steep growth curve.

"New conservation strategies are needed to protect grassland habitats," concludes the report, which is published today in the October issue of BioScience Magazine.

Approximately 147 liters of water are required to grow and refine enough corn to make a single liter of ethanol, according to the study, which highlighted concerns like nutrient depletion and continuous crop rotations on corn ethanol farms.

The authors recommend that producers rely on native prairie grasses, increasingly recognized as a feedstock for biomass and cellulosic ethanol producers, and adopt harvest management techniques to minimize harm to wildlife and watercourses.

When Solar Panels Became Job Killers

BY KEITH BRADSHER | APRIL 8, 2017

WUHAN, CHINA — Russell Abney raised two children on solar power. The 49-year-old Georgia Tech graduate worked for the last decade in Perrysburg, Ohio, a suburb of Toledo, pulling a good salary as an equipment engineer for the largest American solar-panel maker.

On the other side of the world, Gao Song boasted his own solar success story. A former organic fruit retailer who lives in the dusty Chinese city of Wuhan, he installed solar panels on his roof four years ago and found it so lucrative that he went into business installing them for others. By last summer, he and a team of 50 employees were installing solar-panel systems on nearly 100 roofs a month.

Then China shook the global solar business — and transformed both their lives.

"A small vibration back in China," said Frank Haugwitz, a longtime solar industry consultant in Beijing, "can cause an avalanche in prices around the world."

Late last summer, Chinese officials began publicly toying with slashing the subsidies they offer domestic solar-panel buyers. Mr. Gao's business dried up, and he laid off half his workers. "I have been working hard and was just off to a good start," he said. "Now I have to start over."

China's solar-panel makers cut their prices by more than a quarter to compensate, sending global prices plummeting. Western companies found themselves unable to compete, and cut jobs from Germany to Michigan to Texas and points beyond.

Those points included Perrysburg — where Mr. Abney and about 450 other employees suddenly found themselves out of work. "Within just a few months, it all came crashing down," Mr. Abney said. "It's like a death in the family. People feel awkward talking about it."

President Trump, who pressed President Xi Jinping of China on

Workers for Wuhan Guangsheng Photovoltaic Company installing solar panels on a roof in Wuhan, China. China is home to two-thirds of the world's solar-production capacity, and buys half of the world's new solar panels.

trade and other issues this week when they met at Mar-a-Lago in Palm Beach, Fla., has vowed to end what he calls China's unfair business practices. Much of his oratory has involved old-fashioned smokestack industries like steel — industries in which the jobs were already disappearing even before the rise of China.

But economists and business groups warn that China's industrial ambitions have entered a new, far-reaching phase. With its deep government pockets, growing technical sophistication and a comprehensive plan to free itself from dependence on foreign companies, China aims to become dominant in industries of the future like renewable energy, big data and self-driving cars.

With solar, it has already happened. China is now home to two-thirds of the world's solar-production capacity. The efficiency with which its products convert sunlight into electricity is increasingly close to that of panels made by American, German and South Korean companies. Because China also buys half of the world's new solar panels, it now effectively controls the market.

For much of the past century, the ups and downs of the American economy could spell the difference between employment or poverty for people like Chilean copper miners and Malaysian rubber farmers. Now China's policy shifts and business decisions can have the same kind of global impact once wielded by power brokers in Washington, New York and Detroit.

The story of China's rise in solar panels illustrates the profound difficulties the country presents to Mr. Trump, or to any American president. Its size and fast-moving economy give it the ability to redefine industries almost on a dime. Its government-led pursuit of dominance in crucial industries presents a direct challenge to countries where leaders generally leave business decisions to the businesses themselves.

Already, China is the world's largest maker and buyer of steel, cars and smartphones. While it does not necessarily dominate those industries, its government ministries are moving to replicate that success with robots, chips and software — just as in solar.

Chinese panel makers "have the capital, they have the technology, they have the scale," said Ocean Yuan, the chief executive of Grape Solar, a distributor of solar panels based in Eugene, Ore. Of American rivals, he said, "they will crush them."

ROOTED IN FISH

Before he became one of the solar industry's most powerful players, Liu Hanyuan raised fish.

The son of peasants from China's hardscrabble southwest, Mr. Liu sold some of the family's pigs in 1983 for what was then around $100 to buy some fish. Soon he went into the even more lucrative business of selling fish feed, and he eventually moved into pig feed and duck feed. The brand name, Keli, is a combination of the first and last Chinese characters from a famous paraphrasing of Karl Marx by Deng Xiaoping, the father of modern China: Science and technology are primary productive forces.

According to Mr. Liu's authorized biography, he faced local criticism at first for his early embrace of capitalism, and responded by saying that his fish feed was an improved product that followed Deng's dictum. "When my business grows bigger," he said at the time, "I will build another floor for labs."

Plans to shift into computer chips did not pan out, so by 2006, he shifted to solar technology, after taking control of a company that made chemicals for the production of polysilicon, the crystalline raw material for solar panels. That move proved fortunate: China was just then embarking on a concerted effort to become a solar-industry powerhouse.

Over the next six years, Beijing pushed state-owned banks to provide at least $18 billion in loans at low-interest rates to solar-panel manufacturers, and encouraged local governments to subsidize them with cheap land. China had more on its mind than just dominating solar exports: Its severe pollution problems and concerns that rising sea levels from climate change could devastate its teeming coastal cities lent urgency to efforts to develop green technology. At the same time, China also became a major player in wind power through similar policies.

With ample assistance, China's solar-power production capacity expanded more than tenfold from 2007 to 2012. Now six of the top 10 solar-panel makers are Chinese, including the top two, compared with none a decade ago. The solar division of Mr. Liu's company, the Tongwei Group, which discloses few financial details, is one of the fastest-expanding players in the industry.

That growth forced many American and European solar-panel manufacturers into a headlong retreat. Two dozen of them filed for bankruptcy or cut back operations during President Barack Obama's first term, damaging the heady optimism then about clean energy.

In 2012 and 2013, the United States and the European Union concluded that Chinese solar-panel makers were collecting government subsidies and dumping panels, or selling them for less than the cost of producing and shipping them. Both imposed import limits. Chinese manufacturers and officials denied improper subsidies and dumping, and still do.

Several large Chinese manufacturers that had previously overexpanded and had been selling at heavy losses for years then closed their doors. But Western solar companies say Chinese banks still lent heavily to the survivors despite low loan-recovery rates from the defaults of big Chinese solar companies like Suntech, Chaori and LDK Solar.

"The main subsidy is massive, below-market loans by Chinese state-owned commercial banks to finance new capacity and also the massive ongoing losses of Chinese companies," said Jürgen Stein, the president of American operations for SolarWorld, a big German panel maker.

Li Junfeng, a top architect of China's renewable-energy policies until he retired from that responsibility in early January, said that the West had exaggerated the role of the state in helping to finance Chinese solar-panel manufacturers. "The market can decide for itself," he said. "The good companies can get money, the bad companies cannot."

HIGH-TECH HOPES

Like the Chinese solar industry as a whole, Tongwei is thinking bigger.

Mr. Liu's company bought an enormous solar-panel manufacturing complex in central China in 2013 from LDK Solar, which had run into severe financial difficulties. Now it plans to build factories of five gigawatts apiece in the Chinese cities of Chengdu and Hefei. By comparison, the entire global market is only about 77 gigawatts each year, while world capacity is 139 gigawatts.

At the same time, Mr. Liu is dismissive of companies in the West that pioneered many solar technologies but have lost their market shares to China. "They are very jealous," he said, "and cannot catch up with China's pace."

From an environmental standpoint, China's solar push has been good for the world. Solar-panel prices have fallen close to 90 percent over the past decade. Many of the solar panels in America's backyards and solar power plants are made by Chinese companies.

But for the solar industry, Chinese expansion could mean an extended period of low prices and cutbacks for everybody else.

"The solar industry is facing again, I would say, a new winter," said Patrick Pouyanné, the chairman and chief executive of Total, the French oil and gas giant, which owns a controlling stake in SunPower, an American solar-panel maker.

China now hopes to replicate its solar industry's growth in other areas.

Under a plan called Made in China 2025, China hopes to become largely self-sufficient within seven years in a long list of industries, including aircraft, high-speed trains, computer chips and robots. The plan echoes the solar-panel and wind-turbine buildup a decade ago, but with a larger checkbook. Made in China 2025 calls for roughly $300 billion in financial backing: inexpensive loans from state-owned banks, investment funds to acquire foreign technologies, and extensive research subsidies.

If successful, Made in China 2025 would represent a fundamental shift in how China deals with the world. Initially, most of the industries that moved to China, such as shoe and clothing production, were already leaving the United States anyway. Heavy industries such as steel followed. While the shift was profound — some economists estimate that up to 2.4 million American jobs were lost to China from 1999 to 2011, though others dispute that analysis — China has struggled in some areas like autos to create viable global competitors.

American and European business groups have warned that the China 2025 plan means that a much wider range of Western businesses will face the same kind of government-backed competition that has already transformed the solar industry.

"The policies started in solar and are now starting to infect the higher reaches of the economy with Made in China 2025," said Jeremie Waterman, the president of the China Center at the United States Chamber of Commerce in Washington.

RIPPLES FROM WUHAN

In the end, China did not slash subsidies for rooftop solar panels, and cut them only slightly for large power-plant arrays. But prices barely rebounded from last year's slump.

Mr. Gao, of Wuhan, is a slender 37-year-old whose dark hair is already thinning. He said that his business had depended not on homeowners but on profit-minded investors who made use of the subsidies.

The investors would pay three-fifths of the cost of a homeowner's system. The homeowner would take only enough electricity from the panels to power the home. The investor would sell the rest of the electricity to the grid at a high, government-assisted price.

The suggestion that the government might cut the subsidy, even though the government did not follow through on it, panicked his investors. So they stopped financing further deals.

"They fear that the year after next, they may have nothing," he said. He recently hired four more employees to drum up sales, even as installations creep along at a small fraction of demand a year ago.

In Perrysburg, Mr. Abney lost his job at First Solar, the largest solar-panel manufacturer based in the United States, and looked in vain for a job in the auto industry in the Toledo area. He ended up taking a job three weeks ago at a building materials company in Lancaster, Pa. His daughter is going off to college in the autumn, while his wife and son, a high school freshman now, will follow him to central Pennsylvania this summer.

"It's hardest on him because we're pulling him away from his high school and his activities," Mr. Abney said.

First Solar struggled with improving Chinese technology as well as dropping prices.

It laid off workers in Perrysburg partly because it decided not to produce its Series 5 generation of panels, which represented a limited

Gao Song, owner of the solar company Wuhan Guangsheng Photovoltaic Company, using a drone to inspect a rooftop where his workers were installing solar panels.

improvement over its existing Series 4 panels. First Solar, to better compete with Chinese producers, will wait for its lower-cost, high-efficiency Series 6 panels to be ready for production in 2018. In the end, First Solar, which is based in Tempe, Ariz., laid off 1,600 people worldwide.

"It's just kind of a shock factor when a lot of families realize they're no longer going to have a job," said Michael Olmstead, the Republican mayor of Perrysburg.

Though Mr. Abney has started his new job at almost the same pay as his previous one, he says part of him pined for the days when the United States still led in solar energy, and when First Solar was at the forefront of that leadership.

"They were good for us," he said. "And it was great while it lasted."

For Those Near, the Miserable Hum of Clean Energy: The Fight Over Wind Power in Vinalhaven

BY TOM ZELLER JR. | OCTOBER 5, 2010

VINALHAVEN, ME. — Like nearly all of the residents on this island in Penobscot Bay, Art Lindgren and his wife, Cheryl, celebrated the arrival of three giant wind turbines late last year. That was before they were turned on.

"In the first 10 minutes, our jaws dropped to the ground," Mr. Lindgren said. "Nobody in the area could believe it. They were so loud."

Now, the Lindgrens, along with a dozen or so neighbors living less than a mile from the $15 million wind facility here, say the industrial whoosh-and-whoop of the 123-foot blades is making life in this otherwise tranquil corner of the island unbearable.

MATT MCINNIS FOR THE NEW YORK TIMES

Art Lindgren measured noise levels at a wind turbine near Vinalhaven, Me. He and neighbors say the turbines have robbed their community of its tranquility.

They are among a small but growing number of families and homeowners across the country who say they have learned the hard way that wind power — a clean alternative to electricity from fossil fuels — is not without emissions of its own.

Lawsuits and complaints about turbine noise, vibrations and subsequent lost property value have cropped up in Illinois, Texas, Pennsylvania, Wisconsin and Massachusetts, among other states.

In one case in DeKalb County, Ill., at least 38 families have sued to have 100 turbines removed from a wind farm there. A judge rejected a motion to dismiss the case in June.

Like the Lindgrens, many of the people complaining the loudest are reluctant converts to the antiwind movement.

"The quality of life that we came here for was quiet," Mrs. Lindgren said. "You don't live in a place where you have to take an hour-and-15-minute ferry ride to live next to an industrial park. And that's where we are right now."

The wind industry has long been dogged by a vocal minority bearing all manner of complaints about turbines, from routine claims that they ruin the look of pastoral landscapes to more elaborate allegations that they have direct physiological impacts like rapid heart beat, nausea and blurred vision caused by the ultra-low-frequency sound and vibrations from the machines.

For the most extreme claims, there is little independent backing.

Last year, the American Wind Energy Association, a trade group, along with its Canadian counterpart, assembled a panel of doctors and acoustical professionals to examine the potential health impacts of wind turbine noise. In a paper published in December, the panel concluded that "there is no evidence that the audible or sub-audible sounds emitted by wind turbines have any direct adverse physiological effects."

A separate study financed by the Energy Department concluded late last year that, in aggregate, property values were unaffected by nearby wind turbines.

Numerous studies also suggest that not everyone will be bothered by turbine noise, and that much depends on the context into which the noise is introduced. A previously quiet setting like Vinalhaven is more likely to produce irritated neighbors than, say, a mixed-use suburban setting where ambient noise is already the norm.

Of the 250 new wind farms that have come online in the United States over the last two years, about dozen or so have generated significant noise complaints, according to Jim Cummings, the founder of the Acoustic Ecology Institute, an online clearinghouse for information on sound-related environmental issues.

In the Vinalhaven case, an audio consultant hired by the Maine Department of Environmental Protection determined last month that the 4.5-megawatt facility was, at least on one evening in mid-July when Mr. Lindgren collected sound data, in excess of the state's nighttime sound limits. The developer of the project, Fox Island Wind, has contested that finding, and negotiations with state regulators are continuing.

MATT MCINNIS FOR THE NEW YORK TIMES

Residents living less than a mile from the $15 million wind facility in Vinalhaven, Me., say the industrial whoosh-and-whoop of the 123-foot blades is making life unbearable.

In the moonlit woods behind a neighbor's property on a recent evening, Mr. Lindgren, a retired software engineer, clenched a small flashlight between his teeth and wrestled with a tangle of cables and audio recording equipment he uses to collect sound samples for filing complaints.

At times, the rustle of leaves was all that could be heard. But when the surface wind settled, a throbbing, vaguely jetlike sound cut through the nighttime air. "Right there," Mr. Lindgren declared. "That would probably be out of compliance."

Maine, along with many other states, puts a general limit on nighttime noise at 45 decibels — roughly equivalent to the sound of a humming refrigerator. A normal conversation is in the range of 50 to 60 decibels.

In almost all cases, it is not mechanical noise arising from the central gear box or nacelle of a turbine that residents react to, but rather the sound of the blades, which in modern turbines are mammoth appendages well over 100 feet long, as they slice through the air.

Turbine noise can be controlled by reducing the rotational speed of the blades. But the turbines on Vinalhaven already operate that way after 7 p.m., and George Baker, the chief executive of Fox Island Wind — a for-profit arm of the island's electricity co-operative — said that turning the turbines down came at an economic cost.

"The more we do that, the higher goes the price of electricity on the island," he said.

A common refrain among homeowners grappling with sound issues, however, is that they were not accurately informed about the noise ahead of time. "They told us we wouldn't hear it, or that it would be masked by the sound of the wind blowing through the trees," said Sally Wylie, a former schoolteacher down the road from the Lindgrens. "I feel duped."

Similar conflicts are arising in Canada, Britain and other countries. An appeals court in Rennes, France, recently ordered an eight-turbine wind farm to shut down between 10 p.m. and 7 a.m. so residents could get some sleep.

Richard R. James, an acoustic expert hired by residents of Vinalhaven to help them quantify the noise problem, said there was a simpler solution: Do not put the turbines so close to where people live.

"It would seem to be time for the wind utility developers to rethink their plans for duplicating these errors and to focus on locating wind turbines in areas where there is a large buffer zone of about a mile and one-quarter between the turbines and people's homes," said Mr. James, the principal consultant with E-Coustic Solutions, based in Michigan.

Vinalhaven's wind farm enjoys support among most residents, from ardent supporters of all clean energy to those who simply say the turbines have reduced their power bills. Deckhands running the ferry sport turbine pins on their hats, and bumper stickers seen on the island declare "Spin, Baby, Spin."

"The majority of us like them," said Jeannie Conway, who works at the island's ferry office.

But that is cold comfort for Mrs. Lindgren and her neighbors, who say their corner of the island will never be the same.

"I remember the sound of silence so palpable, so merciless in its depths, that you could almost feel your heart stop in sympathy," she said. "Now we are prisoners of sonic effluence. I grieve for the past."

As Demand for Electricity Increases, China Sticks With Nuclear Power

BY KEITH BRADSHER | OCTOBER 14, 2011

MELTDOWNS OF THREE reactors at the Fukushima Daiichi nuclear power plant in Japan last March have put a chill on much of the world's nuclear power industry — but not in China.

The German Parliament voted this summer to close the country's remaining nuclear power plants by 2022, while the Swiss Parliament voted this summer to phase nuclear power out by 2034. Economic stagnation in the United States and most other industrialized economies since 2008 has produced stagnant electricity demand, further sapping interest in nuclear power.

In Japan itself, the government has put on hold its plans to build further nuclear power plants, and the government faces a political battle to continue operating existing reactors. Emerging economies like Brazil and particularly India are still planning nuclear reactors. But the Indian leaders introduced legislation on Sept. 7 that is supposed to increase the independence of nuclear regulators from the industry, though critics are skeptical.

That leaves China poised to build more nuclear reactors in the coming years than the rest of the world combined. But questions abound whether China will be a savior for the international nuclear power industry, or a ferocious competitor that could create even greater challenges for nuclear power companies in the West.

Chinese regulators performed a four-month review of safety at all existing nuclear reactors and reactors under construction after the Fukushima meltdowns and declared them safe. Safety reviews continue at reactors where construction had not yet started at the time of the Fukushima accident.

Jiang Kejun, a director of the Energy Research Institute at the National Development and Reform Commission, the top Chinese economic planning agency, said that the government was sticking to its target of 50 gigawatts of nuclear power by 2015, compared to just 10.8 gigawatts at the end of last year.

Mr. Jiang said in an interview that nuclear power construction targets for 2020 had not yet been set and might end up slightly lower than they would have been without the meltdowns in Fukushima. But he and other Chinese officials say that China's rapidly rising electricity consumption makes nuclear power essential. They even try to portray the Fukushima incidents as salutary for the nuclear power industry, a view seldom heard elsewhere.

"Globally, I think Fukushima could be a good thing for nuclear power," Mr. Jiang said. "We can learn a lot from that. We can't be smug or too clever."

China allowed existing reactors to continue operating during the safety review from March to July and allowed construction to continue at reactors where it had already begun. Chinese regulators have also encouraged electric utilities to continue planning future nuclear power plants.

But one category of reactor has been delayed by the Fukushima incident. At reactors that had been approved before the Fukushima accident but where construction had not yet begun, the government still has not allowed construction to start while continuing to study whether further safety improvements can be made, said Xu Yuanhui, one of China's top nuclear engineers for the past half century.

The delay applies to several conventional nuclear reactors plus Beijing's project to build two reactors in northeastern China, using a new generation of technology known as a pebble-bed design. Critics and advocates describe it as safer than current reactors, though its cost-effectiveness unclear.

The two reactors in Shidao, in Shandong Province in northeast China, were approved days before the Fukushima nuclear accident began with an earthquake and tsunami March 11. But the 50-month timetable for building them cannot start until the government lifts its hold on construction.

"By the end of this year, maybe we'll have some information from the government side," Dr. Xu said.

Nuclear power represented only 1.1 percent of China's electricity generation capacity at the end of last year. With wind turbines and coal-fired power plants being installed at rates that far surpass those in any other country, nuclear power is on track to account for no more than 4 percent of electricity capacity by 2015.

A big part of the appeal of nuclear energy for Chinese officials is that it supplies baseload power, meaning it is available 24 hours a day and seven days a week to meet needs. China passed the United States last year as the world's largest installer of wind turbines, but wind still accounts for only 3.2 percent of China's installed electricity generation capacity and less than 2 percent of electricity generated.

Coal remains by far the dominant source of electricity in China, producing three-quarters of the country's electricity. Nuclear power mainly displaces coal as a source of baseload power. That has also made it popular with Chinese officials, as they have set increasingly ambitious targets to slow the country's rapid rise in emissions of global warming gases, in which the country already leads the world.

Until reliable, large-scale storage of electricity is perfected for renewable energy sources like the wind and sun, "they've got to continue using nuclear as a fundamental part of their fuel mix," said James A. Maguire, the regional managing director for Asian infrastructure at Aon Risk Solutions, a risk management and insurance broker.

Coal is the most polluting major source of electricity in terms of emissions of climate-changing gases, while nuclear power is one of the cleanest. Coal mining accidents also kill more than 2,000 people a year in China, and large areas of the countryside in northern China have been heavily polluted.

China is paying particular attention to nuclear safety issues, however, because it has some of the world's most densely populated rural areas. If a nuclear accident rendered even a small area around a power plant uninhabitable, many would need to be resettled.

China now has an unusually varied fleet of nuclear reactors, using French, American, Russian and homegrown technology. While awarding contracts to a wide range of multinational nuclear power plant contractors, it has required that they provide documentation on exactly how to build the reactors.

That will give China the ability to export reactors in a few years, in competition with industrialized nations, nuclear power industry experts warned. Demand outside China could revive if memories of the Fukushima accident fade or if worries about global warming become more pressing.

China is not only acquiring technology. It is also creating economies of scale by building dozens of reactors at the same time. As a population equal to New York City's moves into China's cities each year demanding air-conditioners and other electricity-guzzling conveniences, consumption is likely to continue growing by double digits.

"It's the largest migration in history, so they need to build a lot of infrastructure," said Dennis Bracy, the chief executive of the U.S.-China Clean Energy Forum, a bilateral discussion group formed by the Chinese government with prominent Americans from previous Republican and Democratic administrations. "I believe they will stay with nuclear as part of the portfolio."

Glossary

adiabatic The quality of something occurring without gaining or losing heat.

arbiter Someone whose opinion or judgment carries great authority.

biomass Organic matter used as a fuel, especially in a power station for generating electricity.

carbon A naturally abundant, nonmetallic element that occurs in all organic compounds and can be found in all known forms of life.

consortium An agreement or other association between two or more businesses.

deforestation The act of clearing all the trees from a wide area.

duped To be easily fooled or cheated.

emissions An amount of something, especially a gas that harms the environment, that is sent out into the air.

ethanol A type of fuel made with ethyl alcohol, used as a biofuel additive to gasoline.

fossil fuel A natural fuel such as coal or gas, formed in the geological past from the remains of living organisms.

fracking The process of injecting liquid at high pressure into subterranean rocks, boreholes, etc. so as to force open existing fissures and extract oil or gas.

geothermal Relating to the use of heat from the Earth's interior.

greenhouse gas A gas like carbon dioxide or methane that absorbs infrared radiation, trapping heat in the atmosphere.

grid parity When an alternative energy source provides power at a cost that is less than or equal to the price of the same amount of power provided by the electricity grid.

hydraulic Moved, operated or otherwise effected using water.

idyllic Picturesque or delightful, particularly of a time or a place.

imposition The act of enforcing or inflicting something unwanted upon another party.

particulate Something in the form of a very small particle, such as dust or soot.

photovoltaic Something that produces electric voltage or current, espcially through the light of the sun.

sustainability Related to using a resource in such a way so that it does not permanently run out or become irreparably damaged.

turbine A machine that uses a wheel or rotor moving through a fast-moving flow of water, steam, gas, air or other fluid to create power.

Media Literacy Terms

"Media literacy" refers to the ability to access, understand, critically assess and create media. The following terms are important components of media literacy, and they will help you critically engage with the articles in this title.

attribution The method by which a source is identified or by which facts and information are assigned to the person who provided them.

bias A disposition of prejudice in favor of a certain idea, person or perspective.

byline Name of the writer, usually placed between the headline and the story.

caption Identifying copy for a picture; also called a legend or cutline.

chronological order Method of writing a story presenting the details of the story in the order in which they occurred.

column Type of story that is a regular feature, often on a recurring topic, written by the same journalist, generally known as a columnist.

credibility The quality of being trustworthy and believable, said of a journalistic source.

ceditorial Article of opinion or interpretation.

fake news A fictional or made-up story presented in the style of a legitimate news story, intended to deceive readers; also commonly used as an insult to criticize legitimate news that one dislikes because of its perspective or unfavorable coverage of a subject.

feature story Article designed to entertain as well as to inform.

headline Type, usually 18 point or larger, used to introduce a story.

human interest story Type of story that focuses on individuals and how events or issues affect their life, generally offering a sense of relatability to the reader.

impartiality Principle of journalism that a story should not reflect a journalist's bias and should contain balance.

interview story Type of story in which the facts are gathered primarily by interviewing another person or persons.

inverted pyramid Method of writing a story using facts in order of importance, beginning with a lead and then gradually adding paragraphs in order of relevance from most interesting to least interesting.

news story An article or style of expository writing that reports news, generally in a straightforward fashion and without editorial comment.

op-ed An opinion piece that reflects a prominent journalist's opinion on topic of interest.

paraphrase The summary of an individual's words, with attribution, rather than a direct quotation of their exact words.

plagiarism An attempt to pass another person's work as one's own without attribution.

quotation The use of an individual's exact words indicated by the use of quotation marks and proper attribution.

style A distinctive use of language in writing or speech; also a news or publishing organization's rules for consistent use of language with regards to spelling, punctuation, typography and capitalization, usually regimented by a house style guide.

tone A manner of expression in writing or speech.

Media Literacy
Questions

1. Identify the various sources cited in the article "Fuel Without the Fossil" (on page 10). How does the journalist attribute information to each of these sources in his article? How effective are his attributions in helping the reader identify his sources?

2. In "Race Is On to Clean Up Hydraulic Fracturing" (on page 35), Erica Gies directly quotes Charles Vinick of Ecosphere Technologies. What are the strengths of using direct quotes as opposed to paraphrasing? What are the weaknesses?

3. Compare the headlines of "Public Lives; A Windmill Builder, Tilting at the Old Ways" (on page 48) and "Why a Big Utility is Embracing Wind and Solar" (on page 134). Which is a more compelling headline, and why? How could the less compelling headline be changed to better draw the reader's interest?

4. What type of story is "For Those Near, the Miserable Hum of Clean Energy" (on page 202)? Can you identify another article in this collection that is the same type of story?

5. Does Erica Gies demonstrate the journalistic principle of impartiality in her article "Race Is On to Clean Up Hydraulic Fracturing" (on page 35)? If so, how did she do so? If not, what could she have included to make her article more impartial?

6. The article "The Connection Between Cleaner Air and Longer Lives" (on page 32) is an example of an op-ed. Identify how Michael

Greenstone's attitude and tone help convey his opinion on the topic.

7. Does "Cleaner China Coal May Still Feed Global Warming" (on page 44) use multiple sources? What are the strengths of using multiple sources in a journalistic piece? What are the weaknesses of relying heavily on one source/few sources?

8. "Public Lives; A Windmill Builder, Tilting at the Old Ways" (on page 48) is an example of an interview. What are the benefits of providing readers with direct quotes of an interviewed subject's speech? Is the subject of an interview always a reliable source?

9. What is the intention of the article "The Connection Between Cleaner Air and Longer Lives" (on page 32)? How effectively does it achieve its intended purpose?

10. Analyze the authors' positions in "When Solar Panels Became Job Killers" (on page 194) and "Solar Trade Case, With Trump as Arbiter, Could Upend Market" (on page 187). Do you think one journalist is more balanced or impartial in their reporting than the other? If so, why do you think so?

11. Identify each of the sources in "When Solar Panels Became Job Killers" (on page 194) as a primary source or a secondary source. Evaluate the reliability and credibility of each sources. How does your evaluation of each source change your perspective on this article?

Citations

All citations in this list are formatted according to the Modern Language Association's (MLA) style guide.

BOOK CITATION

NEW YORK TIMES EDITORIAL STAFF, THE. *Clean Energy: The Economics of a Growing Market.* New York: New York Times Educational Publishing, 2019.

ARTICLE CITATIONS

BARRINGER, FELICITY. "Warren Buffett's Big Bet on Renewables in Nevada." *The New York Times*, 7 Oct. 2014, https://www.nytimes.com/2014/10/08/business/energy-environment/warren-buffetts-big-bet-on-renewables-in-nevada.html?ref=businessspecial2.

BRADSHER, KEITH. "Clean Power That Reaps a Whirlwind." *The New York Times*, 9 May 2007, https://www.nytimes.com/2007/05/09/business/09carbon.html.

BRADSHER, KEITH. "Cleaner China Coal May Still Feed Global Warming." *The New York Times*, 17 Jun. 2011, https://archive.nytimes.com/query.nytimes.com/gst/fullpage-9502EFDC153FF934A25755C0A9679D8B63.html.

BRADSHER, KEITH. "As Demand for Electricity Increases, China Sticks With Nuclear Power." *The New York Times*, 14 Oct. 2011, https://archive.nytimes.com/query.nytimes.com/gst/fullpage-9C05E0D91439F937A25753C1A9679D8B63.html.

BRADSHER, KEITH. "Paying in Pollution for Energy Hunger." *The New York Times*, 9 Jan, 2007, https://www.nytimes.com/2007/01/09/business/worldbusiness/09village.html.

BRADSHER, KEITH. "When Solar Panels Became Job Killers." *The New York Times*, 8 Apr. 2017, https://www.nytimes.com/2017/04/08/business/china-trade-solar-panels.html.

BRENHOUSE, HILLARY. "Canada Produces Strain of Algae for Fuel." *The New York Times*, 29 Sept. 2010, https://www.nytimes.com/2014/10/08/business/energy-environment/airlines-fly-the-skies-on-a-sugar-high.html.

BRENHOUSE, HILLARY. "If Earth Were Powered From Space." *The New York Times*, 12 Oct. 2010, https://www.nytimes.com/2010/10/13/business/energy-environment/13iht-renspace.html.

BRENHOUSE, HILLARY. "Indonesia Seeks to Tap Its Huge Geothermal Reserves." *The New York Times*, 26 July 2010, https://www.nytimes.com/2010/07/27/business/global/27iht-renindo.html.

CARDWELL, DIANE. "Fight to Keep Alternative Energy Local Stymies an Industry." *The New York Times*, 23 Mar. 2016, https://www.nytimes.com/2016/03/24/business/energy-environment/fight-to-keep-alternative-energy-local-stymies-an-industry.html.

CARDWELL, DIANE. "Fuel From Landfill Methane Goes on Sale." *The New York Times*, 2 Oct. 2013, https://www.nytimes.com/2013/10/03/business/energy-environment/the-swamp-gas-station-fuel-from-landfill-methane-goes-on-sale.html.

CARDWELL, DIANE. "Solar Trade Case, With Trump as Arbiter, Could Upend Market." *The New York Times*, 30 June 2017, https://www.nytimes.com/2017/06/30/business/energy-environment/solar-energy-trade-china-trump.html.

GARDINER, BETH. "The Challenges of Cleaning Up Cooking." *The New York Times*, 8 Dec. 2015, https://www.nytimes.com/2015/12/09/business/energy-environment/the-challenges-of-cleaning-up-cooking.html.

GARDINER, BETH. "Harnessing the Net to Power a Green Revolution." *The New York Times*, 18 Jun. 2013, https://www.nytimes.com/2013/06/19/business/energy-environment/harnessing-the-net-to-power-a-green-revolution.html.

GELLES, DAVID. "How Producing Clean Power Turned Out to Be a Messy Business." *The New York Times*, 13 Aug. 2016, https://www.nytimes.com/2016/08/14/business/energy-environment/how-producing-clean-power-turned-out-to-be-a-messy-business.html.

GIES, ERICA. "The Challenge of Storing Energy on a Large Scale." *The New York Times*, 29 Sept. 2010, https://www.nytimes.com/2010/09/30/business/energy-environment/30iht-renstore.html.

GIES, ERICA. "The Race is On to Clean Up Hydraulic Fracturing." *The New York Times*, 4 Dec. 2012, https://www.nytimes.com/2012/12/05/business/

energy-environment/race-is-on-to-clean-up-hydraulic-fracturing.html.

GILLIS, JUSTIN AND HAL HARVEY. "Why a Big Utility Is Embracing Wind and Solar." *The New York Times*, 6 Feb. 2018, https://www.nytimes.com/2018/02/06/opinion/utility-embracing-wind-solar.html.

GREENSTONE, MICHAEL. "The Connection Between Cleaner Air and Longer Lives." *The New York Times*, 24 Sept. 2015, https://www.nytimes.com/2015/09/25/upshot/the-connection-between-cleaner-air-and-longer-lives.html.

HAYES, DAVID J. "Clean Power, Off the Grid." *The New York Times*, 17 Jul. 2014, https://www.nytimes.com/2014/07/18/opinion/wind-solar-clean-power-off-the-grid.html.

KILGANNON, COREY. "Public Lives; A Windmill Builder, Tilting at the Old Ways." *The New York Times*, 30 Jan. 2003, https://www.nytimes.com/2003/01/30/nyregion/public-lives-a-windmill-builder-tilting-at-the-old-ways.html.

LOFTUS, LOUISE. "Vast Potential in the Discomfort of Howling Winds." *The New York Times*, 29 Sept. 2010, https://www.nytimes.com/2010/09/30/business/energy-environment/30iht-renscot.html.

LORINC, JOHN. "Reconciling Clean Energy and Conservation." *The New York Times*, 1 Oct. 2009, https://green.blogs.nytimes.com/2009/10/01/reconciling-clean-energy-and-conservation/.

NESBIT, JEFF. "Coal's Continuing Decline." *The New York Times*, 19 Feb. 2018, https://www.nytimes.com/2018/02/19/opinion/trump-coal-decline.html.

PLUMER, BRAD. "Kelp Farms and Mammoth Windmills Are Just Two of the Government's Long-Shot Energy Bets." *The New York Times*, 16 Mar. 2018, https://www.nytimes.com/2018/03/16/climate/arpa-e-summit.html.

REED, STANLEY. "From Oil to Solar: Saudi Arabia Plots a Shift to Renewables." *The New York Times*, 5 Feb. 2018, https://www.nytimes.com/2018/02/05/business/energy-environment/saudi-arabia-solar-renewables.html.

ROSENTHAL, ELISABETH. "No Furnaces But Heat Aplenty in 'Passive Houses'." *The New York Times*, 26 Dec. 2008, https://www.nytimes.com/2008/12/27/world/europe/27house.html.

WALD, MATTHEW L. "Fuel Without the Fossil." *The New York Times*, 9 Nov. 2007, www.nytimes.com/2007/11/09/business/09fuel.html.

WALD, MATTHEW L. "How Grid Efficiency Went South." *The New York Times*, 7 Oct. 2014, https://www.nytimes.com/2014/10/08/business/energy-environment/how-grid-efficiency-went-south-.html.

YEE, AMY. "Airlines Fly the Skies on Sugar High." *The New York Times*, 7 Oct. 2014, https://www.nytimes.com/2014/10/08/business/energy-environment/airlines-fly-the-skies-on-a-sugar-high.html.

YEE, AMY. "Geothermal Energy Grows in Kenya." *The New York Times*, 23 Feb. 2018, https://www.nytimes.com/2018/02/23/business/geothermal-energy-grows-in-kenya.html.

ZELLER, TOM, JR. "For Those Near, the Miserable Hum of Clean Energy." *The New York Times*, 5 Oct. 2010, https://www.nytimes.com/2010/10/06/business/energy-environment/06noise.html.

ZELLER, TOM, JR. "Trading Pumps for Plugs: We Aren't There Yet." *The New York Times*, 30 Mar. 2011, https://www.nytimes.com/2011/03/31/business/31ELECTRIC.html.

Index